Learn to play Taiji Quan with

看图学
太极拳

戈金刚◎主编
蒋敏洁◎演示

汉英对照

北京科学技术出版社

图书在版编目 (CIP) 数据

看图学太极拳（汉英对照）／戈金刚，蒋敏洁主编．
－北京：北京科学技术出版社，2009.3　　重印
ISBN 978-7-5304-3674-5

Ⅰ．看…　Ⅱ．①戈…②蒋…　Ⅲ．太极拳－图解
Ⅳ．G852.11-64

中国版本图书馆 CIP 数据核字（2008）第 033957 号

看图学太极拳（汉英对照）

作　　者：戈金刚　蒋敏洁
翻　　译：戈金刚　蒋敏洁
摄　　影：何智诚
责任编辑：赵　晶
责任校对：黄立辉
责任印制：韩美子
封面设计：回归线视觉传达
图文制作：樊润琴　魏月玲
出 版 人：张敬德
出版发行：北京科学技术出版社
社　　址：北京西直门南大街 16 号
邮政编码：100035
电话传真：0086-10-66161951(总编室)
　　　　　0086-10-66113227(发行部) 0086-10-66161952（发行部传真）
电子信箱：bjkjpress@163.com
网　　址：www.bkjpress.com
经　　销：新华书店
印　　刷：北京捷迅佳彩印刷有限公司
开　　本：720mm×1020mm　1/16
字　　数：200 千
印　　张：8
版　　次：2008 年 6 月第 1 版
印　　次：2009 年 3 月第 3 次印刷
ISBN 978-7-5304-3674-5/G・664

定　价：32.00 元（赠 DVD 光盘）

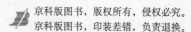

Foreword 前言

中国是一个历史悠久和文化灿烂的国家。中国人民为世界文明作出了许多伟大贡献，太极拳就是其中之一。

太极，是我国古代用以认识和分析事物的思想方法。"太极"这个词，最早见于《易经》。太极是一种哲学概念，是对自然界相互关联的某些事物和现象对立双方的概括。它既可以代表两个相互对立的事物，也可以代表同一事物内部所存在的相互对立的两个方面。

太极拳以"太极"哲理指导拳路，拳路的一招一式又构成了太极图形。拳形为"太极"，拳意亦在"太极"，以太极之动而生阳，静而生阴，激发人体自身的阴阳气血达到"阴平阳秘"的状态，从而使生命保持旺盛的活力。

太极拳不仅能健身、防病，而且更适用于某些慢性疾病的康复。因此，太极拳现已演化成为我国康复医疗的一项重要手段。它不仅造福于中国人民，也造福于全人类。

简化太极拳是由原国家体委于1956年组织部分专家，在大架"杨式太极拳"的基础上，按"由简入繁、循序渐进、易学易记"的原则加以简化、改编的一个太极拳规范套路，全套共分四段24式，所以又称"24式太极拳"。它要求习练者做

China is a nation with a long history and a splendid culture. The Chinese people have made great contributions to the civilization of the world, one of these is Taiji Quan.

The theory of Taiji is a conceptual framework which was used for observing and analysing the material world in ancient China. Taiji first appeared in *The Book of Changes*. Taiji is a philosophical conceptualization, a means to generalize the two opposite principle which maybe observed in all related phenomena within the natural world. They may represent two separate phenomena with opposing natures, as well as different and opposite aspects with the same phenomenon.

The course of Taiji Quan is under the guidance of the philosophical theory of Taiji(infinite void). Every stroke and every posture forms the Taiji diagram. The shape of Taiji Quan is "Taiji" and the intention of Taiji Quan also lies in "Taiji". The movement of Taiji generates Yang, while the motionlessness of Taiji generates Yin, with both of which stimulate qi and blood of the human body itself to reach the state of "Yin is even and well while Yang is firm" and to make life brimming with exuberant vigor.

Taiji Quan(shadow boxing) can be employed to improve one's health and defend oneself; moreover, it is good for rehabilitation from some chronic diseases. It has, therefore, become one of the important means of rehabilitation in China. Taiji Quan benefits not only Chinese people but also the human beings.

In 1956, by some Taiji Quan experts of the former National Sports Committee, a simplified set of Taiji Quan based on the Yang-Style Big Frame was issued, under the principle of being easy to learn and practise, and from simple to complex. This series consists of 24 forms, so it is also called "24 Forms Taiji Quan". It requires concentration, harmony, either empty or solid steps, circular movements and continuity, and even motions. All

到：精神贯注，上下相随，虚实分明，连贯圆活，速度均匀。整套动作如行云流水，连绵不断，充分体现传统太极拳动作的柔和、缓慢、轻灵的特点，是学习太极拳的基础套路，也可用于一般性比赛。简化太极拳历经50多年，实践证明，它是众多太极拳流派中普及率最高、参与人数最多、传播最为广泛的一个套路。全套完整练习一次需4～6分钟。

42式太极拳竞赛套路是1990年中国武术院组织部分专家及著名运动员创编的，它是以杨式太极拳为基础，吸收了陈、吴、孙式太极拳的动作，继承了传统太极拳中绵绵不断、轻松柔和、圆活自然的运动特点，充分突出了太极拳意领身随、刚柔相济的技术要领。这套拳既是国内和国外运动员竞赛的规定套路，同时也是有一定基础的太极拳爱好者的提高套路。此套路完整练习一次需要5分钟左右时间。

太极拳不仅是颐养生命、增强体质、预防疾病，从而延年益寿的一种医事活动，也是一种陶冶性情、追求和谐的高雅文化活动。其天人合一、崇尚自然的理念是一般体育运动所无法替代的。

随着21世纪全球经济文化一体化、信息化时代的到来，崇尚自然，追求和谐、文明与健康的理念更加深入人心，而太极拳运动正是人们实现这一愿望的理想运动方式。现在，太极拳运动已经传播到全世界150多个国家和地区，世界各国习练太极拳的人数已逾数亿，越来越多的国

the movements are slow,like clouds floating in the sky,which gives prominence to its characteristic of softness,slowness and lightness.Simplified Taiji Quan is a basic routine for people to learn Taiji,and also to be used in competition.After 50 years and more of development,it is proved that simplified Taiji Quan is the most popular one in Taiji family.It will take 4~6 minutes to perform the whole routine.

In 1990,by some experts and famous athletes in the Wushu Institute of China,the competition routine of 42 Style Taiji Quan was created based mainly on Yang-Style while synthesizing the movements from several other Taiji Quan style,such as Chen,Wu,Sun.It inherited the characteristics of being continous,slight and soft,and circular and natural in traditional Taiji Quan,as well as gave prominence to technical requirements of movements with comprehension,and stoutness with softness.It is not only a required routine for athletes all over the world,but also one for amateurs to improve their own skills.It will take about 5 minutes to perform the whole routine.

Taiji Quan is not only one of the medical pursuits which cultivates life,builds up health,and prevents diseases so as to achieve the purpose of prolonging life but also an elegant activity to cultivate one's temper and pursue the harmony. It advocates keeping man and universe being a unit and venerates nature,which is far beyond common sports activities.

With the coming of the wholeness of global economy and culture,and the informational times,people much more thirst for cultivation and health than ever.At present,Taiji Quan is spread about 150 countries,and the practicers had been than millions upon millions. Taiji Quan is just the proper way for people to realize their wishes. Thus,more and more practicers who like Taiji Quan are eager to master some therapies of Taiji Quan in order to interchange connotation of Taiji Quan in English language for to establish a good relationship with the alien colleagues;not a few foreign physicians are also eager to master some health preservation in Taiji Quan in order to counteract the weaknesses in Western medicine. There are also other persons who intend to go

内太极拳爱好者迫切需要用英语交流太极拳的内涵，以便更快地与国外同道建立良好的关系；有些国外医师也迫切要求掌握一些太极拳养生方法，以弥补西医治疗的不足；一些准备出国者，对针灸、按摩、气功、太极拳疗法饶有兴趣，以便日后有机会业余为人治病；更有广大的大学在校学生和毕业生希望掌握关于太极拳英语的表达方法，以适应日益增多的国内外文化交流的需要。汉英对照的本书可以为上述读者提供帮助。

本书熔科学性和实用性为一炉，专业内容深入浅出、详略适中，汉英双语行文严谨、准确规范。

为了使习练者能够更加直观、自主地学习，本书配有DVD双语教学光盘，充分运用现代教育技术手段，全面、系统、直观地介绍了简化太极拳和42式太极拳竞赛套路的完整套路和习练方法，对提高学习兴趣和学习效率，以及理解与记忆动作等方面具有独特的作用，可与本书参照学习。

戈金刚

蒋敏洁

abroad,they are quite interested in acupuncture, massage,Qigong and Taiji Quan,for the purpose to obtain the opportunity to treat patients in their spare time in the future.Furthermore,the vast numbers of university students and the graduates from the colleges hope to master correctly the expressive mode of English language so that they are able to meet the requirements of the increasing activities in the domestic and international academic exchange.This edition of "24 Forms and 42 Forms Taiji Quan"is specially written to provide help for these above-mentioned readers.

This book is written scientifically and practically. The complicated professional contents are expressed in a simple and explicit way and both of English and Chinese languages are strict,correct and standard.

To help practiticers learn it directly and on their own responsibility,we made a DVD,in which modern teaching technologies are used to systematically and completely introduce the whole routines and practice methods of Simplified Taiji Quan and Competition Routine of 42-form Taiji Quan.So it helps the practiticers a lot to understand and remember movements,and improves their study efficiency,it'll be a good references for practiticers to learn the book with it.

Ge Jin Gang
Jiang Min Jie

Contents 目录

Part 4　Competition Routine of 42 Forms Taiji Quan

太极拳的主要特点

The Main Features of Taiji Quan

一、轻松柔和

太极拳的架式比较平稳舒展，动作要求不僵不拘，符合人体的生理习惯，并且一般说来，没有忽高忽落的明显变化和激烈的跳跃动作。所以，练习一两遍之后，虽然感到身上微微出汗，但很少发生气喘，练拳之后给人以轻松愉快之感。由于太极拳的这个特点，因而不同年龄、性别和体质的人，都可以练习，尤其对体弱和患有某些慢性疾病的人，更是一种较好的体疗手段。

二、连贯均匀

整套太极拳动作，从"起势"到"收势"，不论动作的虚实变化还是姿势的过渡转换，都是紧密衔接、连贯一气的，看不出有明显停顿的地方。整套动作演练起来，速度均匀，前后贯串，好像行云流水，绵绵不断。

三、圆活自然

太极拳的动作不同于其他拳术，它要求上肢动作处处带有弧形，避免直来直往，这是符合人体各关节自然弯曲状态的。通过弧形活动进行锻炼，有利于动作的圆活自然，体现出柔和的特点，能使身体各部分得到均匀地锻炼。

1. Mildness and Gentleness

The basic stance is steady and unstrained,and the movements should smooth and gentle,without suddenly punches or vigorous leaps.That is why after practising the whole set once or twice, there is hardly any panting,but only a light perspiration over the whole body and a sense of satisfaction.For this reason,Taiji Quan is almost suited to anybody,regardless of age,sex or physique.It is an excellent therapeutic exercise, particularly for the feeble and the chronically diseased.

2. Continuity and Evenness

From beginning to end,all the movements,including shifting of weight and moving from one position to another,are closely linked in an endless chain without a break.They follow one another at an even and unhurried pace like floating clouds or a smooth running stream.

3. Natural and Circular Movement

The style of Taiji Quan distinguishes itself from others by its unique circular movements of the upper limbs,avoiding direct and straight impact,which is in conformity with the natural curvature of bodily joints.The exercise helps shape one's movements into gentle curves with natural grace.

四、协调完整

在太极拳运动中，不论是整个套路，还是单个动作姿势，都要求上下相随，内（意念、呼吸）外（躯干、四肢动作）一体，身体各部分之间要密切配合。打太极拳时，必须以腰为轴，手脚的许多动作都由躯干来带动，并且互相呼应，不要上下脱节或此动彼不动，显得呆滞和支离破碎。

上述的这些特点，决定了太极拳在锻炼方法上对姿势、动作的各种要求。

4. Concord and Consistency

Throughout the exercise,with every single movement or position,the practicer's upper half and lower half,"Inner self"(attention and breath)and"outer slef"(the torso and limbs)must be at one.In fact,there must be perfect coordination of the whole body,with the waist as the main axis.Even the hands and feet have to follow the body without any discord and fragment.

Such are the artistic features of Taiji Quan.

第二部分
Part 2

练习太极拳对身体
各部位姿势的要求

Requirments for position of the whole body

一、头颈

头顶要"悬"。练习太极拳时，对头部姿势的要求是很严格的。所谓"头顶悬"、"虚领顶劲"，或"提顶"、"吊顶"的说法，都是要求习练者头向上顶，但是要避免颈部肌肉硬直，更不要东倒西歪或自由摇晃。头颈动作应随着身体位置和方向的变换，与躯干的旋转上下连贯协调一致。面部要自然，下颏微向里收，口唇自然合闭，舌尖上卷，舔住上腭，以加强唾液的分泌。

二、眼神

眼神要随着身体的转动，注视前手（个别时候看后手）或平视前方，既不可皱眉瞪眼，也不要随意闭眼或精神涣散。打拳时，神态力求自然，注意力集中，以达到最佳的锻炼效果。

三、肩肘

肩要沉、肘要垂。沉肩垂肘是指要做到肩关节放松，自然下沉，不可耸肩。肘关节始终微屈下垂，肘若抬起，肩就不能够下沉。另外，沉肩垂肘时要注意腋下留有余地，不要把胳膊肘贴在肋部，肘与肋之间要空出一拳距离，以使手臂能回旋自如。

1. Head and Neck

When practising Taiji Quan, the position of head must be strictly maintained. "Head erect with neck relaxed" stipulates that the practicer should hold his head upright without straining neck muscles or allowing it to sway. The movement of neck must coordinate with the change in position of body and turning of torso. The facial expression should be natural, chin drawn inward and mouth a bit open or closed naturally with tip of tongue on palate to reinforce secreting saliva.

2. Eyesight

Following the turn of body, the eyes would either rest on the hand in front (in a few cases, on the hand in rear) or look straight ahead without closing or starting in any angry glare. When practising, one must look fully composed and concentrated to achieve the best effects.

3. Shoulder and Elbow

Shoulder should be lower and elbow hang down. Lowering shoulders and hanging elbow mean relaxing these joints down naturally. Don't shrug shoulders, and keep elbows slightly bent always down. If the elbows are raised, the shoulders could not be lower. Besides, when lowering shoulders and hanging elbows down, keep elbow a-fist-width apart from ribs, in order to leave a place in oxter to rotate your arms freely.

四、手腕

手指要舒。 舒指是要做到五指自然分开，手指微屈，掌心微含，虎口成弧形。手指不可并紧也不可松散或软弱无力。

腕要"坐"。 坐腕也叫"塌腕"。要求在手臂运动过程中，腕部既不僵硬，也不软塌，而是柔活有韧性地运转。

五、胸背

胸要含，背要拔。 含胸，指胸肌自然松弛。拔背，指背部舒展开阔。要做到含胸拔背，首先要放松肩锁关节，两肩微向前合，两肋微敛。做到含胸就能达到拔背的要求，从而也可免除胸肋间的紧张，呼吸调节也自然了。

六、腰

在练太极拳的过程中，身体要求端正安舒，不偏不倚，腰部起着重要的作用。过去有人说："腰脊为第一主宰"、"腰如车轴"等等，都说明了如果腰部力量中断或在身体转动中起不了"车轴"的作用，就不可做到周身完整一气。练习时，无论是进退或旋转，凡是由虚而逐渐落实的动作，腰部都要有意识地向下松垂，以帮助气的下沉。注意腰腹不可用力前挺，以免影响转换的灵活性。这样腰部向下松垂，可以增加两腿力量，使下盘得到稳固，使动作既圆活又完整。

七、臀部

要"垂臀"（或称"敛臀"）。这是为了避免臀部凸出而破坏身体的自然形态。练习时，要注意臀部自然下垂，不要左右扭动。在松腰、正脊的要求下，臀部肌肉要有意识地收敛，以维持躯干的正直。总之，垂臀和顶头的要求一样，应用意识调整，不是用力去控制。

4. Palm and Wrist

Fingers should separate.Separating fingers means to separate all fingers naturally,fingers bent a little and palms drawn in a bit,"Tiger mouth"(part of the hand between the thumb and the index finger)forming an arc.Fingers are either closed,too far apart or lack of strength and weakness.

Wrists wants to"sit down".Sitting down wrists is also called relaxing wrists.While moving arms,wrists shouldn't be stiff or disable and should be soft and tenacity in moving.

5. Chest and Back

Keep chest slightly inward,Keep back fully extending.It means chest muscles to stretch freely naturally.If you want to do it,you should relax acromion-clavicular joints first,and slightly close shoulders forward and draw ribs in.Chest in and back fully extending are inseparable.The muscles on chest are relaxed to eliminate tension on ribs and thus ensure natural breathing.

6. Waist

In practising Taiji Quan ,the waist plays a most important role in keeping body erect and at ease.That is why people say,"The waist is the mainstay",and"The lumbar spine is the axis",which means that without the lumbar section as axis or central switch of strength,the movement of the whole body will be in discord. While in practice,whether going forward or backward,or turning,or changing from"empty"to "solid"in movement,keep the waist relaxed so as to conduct"qi"downward.Do not thrust out the belly to ensure freedom in turning or change of position.Besides,the relaxation of the waist will also strengthen the legs,reinforcing the basis of the posture to allow flexibility and sostenutos of movement.

7. Buttocks

In practising Taiji Quan,buttocks should be held"in".Avoid jutting them out and spoiling the natural position,or twisting sideways.With the waist relaxed and spine erect,hold the body straight.But like the head,the buttocks should be kept in position by mental awareness rather than by strength.

八、腿部

在练习太极拳的过程中，进退的变换，发劲的根源和周身的稳定，主要在于腿部。因而在锻炼时，要特别注意重心的移动、脚放的位置和腿弯的程度。练拳人常说："其根在脚，发于腿，主宰于腰，形于手指"，可见腿部动作姿势的好坏，关系着周身姿势的正确与否。

九、裆

裆要圆。裆即会阴部，在打拳过程中要始终裆圆。裆圆的意思是撑开胯根，两膝微向里扣。

十、胯

胯要落。落胯的意思是放松胯关节并稍下沉。腰腿的灵活性受胯的影响。因此练拳的人要经常做弯腰、压腿和高踢腿的动作，这样可以拉长韧带，松开胯关节，提高下肢的灵活性和柔韧性。

十一、膝

膝要活。活膝是指太极拳拳式始终要求处于屈膝和虚实交换运动中。在两腿交替运动中，一条腿几乎支撑全身重量，其中以膝关节的负担重量较大，所以膝关节必须有力而又灵活，才能保证两腿屈伸自如。

十二、足

足要稳。足是根基，足部的动作要稳当、灵活、正确，如果根基不稳，其步型、步法必乱。

8. Legs

In practising Taiji Quan,legs determine the direction,provide the source of strength,and ensure stability of body.Therefore,special care is given to the shifting of weight,the position of either foot and the bending of legs.The practicers often say,"The strength is rooted in the feet,gathered in legs,centered in the waist and shown in the fingers".From this we can see how important the movement and position of the legs.

9. Crotch

The crotch should be circular all the time in practising Taiji Quan.Crotch is perineum. Circular crotch means to open the ends of hips with knees slightly inward.

10. Hips

Hip joints should be relaxed and sunk a bit.They play important role in adjusting the movements of waist and legs.Therefore practicers should bow waist,press legs,and practise high-kick frequently,so as to elongate ligament,relax hip joints.As a result,movements of lower limbs will be more agile and gentle.

11. Knees

Knees should be able to move quickly and easily.In practising Taiji Quan,keep knees bent with either empty or solid steps all the time by the shifting of weight.In such steps,knee joints bear most body weight.Therefore,it is the powerful and agile knee joints that ensure free movements of legs.

12. Feet

Feet must be steady.Because feet are root of the whole body.That fixed feet means movements of feet should be steady,nimble and correct.If the feet are not steady,the stances and footwork must be confused.

备　注

本书图中实线表示下一个动作的右手、右脚的运行路线；虚线表示左手、左脚的运行的路线。

Notes

In the illustrations,paths of the next movements are indicated by arrows drawn in solid lines for the right hand and right foot;and dotted lines for the left hand and left foot.

第三部分
Part 3

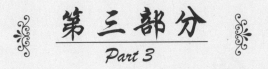

24 Forms Taiji Quan

由简入繁
循序渐进
易学易记

第一组
Series One

1

预备势
Preparatory Posture

1 身体自然站立，两脚并拢，头颈正直，下颌稍内收，胸腹放松，沉肩垂肘，两臂自然下垂，两手轻贴大腿两侧；两眼向前平视；呼吸保持自然。

Stand naturally upright with feet together,hold head and neck erect with chin withdrawn slightly inward,keep chest and abdomen relaxed,hold shoulders and elbows down with arms hanging naturally,hands touching the sides of thighs gently.Eyes looking straight forward and breathing naturally.(Fig.1)

第一式 起势
Form 1 Starting Posture

2 左脚向左开立半步，足距与肩同宽，脚尖向前。

3 两臂慢慢向前平举，两手与肩同高、同宽，双臂自然伸直，两手心向下，指尖向前。

4 两腿慢慢屈膝半蹲,同时两掌轻轻下按至腹前，松肩垂肘坐腕，上体保持正直。

❀ Take half a step to left so that feet are shoulder-width apart,toes pointing forward.(Fig.2)

❀ Raise arms slowly forward,both hands at shoulder level and shoulder-width apart,with arms naturally straight,hearts of hands facing downward with fingertips pointing forward.(Fig.3)

❀ Bend the knees slowly to half squat,while pressing palms gently down to the front of the abdomen,wrists sat and elbows slightly bent,shoulders relaxed,keep the torso upright. (Fig.4)

要 点

　　头颈正直，下颔微向内收，不要故意挺胸或收腹，注意力要集中。两肩下沉，两肘松垂，手指自然微屈。屈膝松腰，臀部不可凸出，重心落于两腿中间。两掌下按要和身体下蹲的动作协调一致。

Points to Remember

Hold the head and neck naturally erect with chin withdrawn slightly inward,do not thrust out chest or withdraw in abdomen intentionally,be fully concentrated,both shoulders are lowered and both elbows hung loose with fingers slightly crooked,body's weight is on both legs.Knees are bent,waist section relaxed and buttocks do not jut out. Lowering of palms should be coordinated with squatting of body.

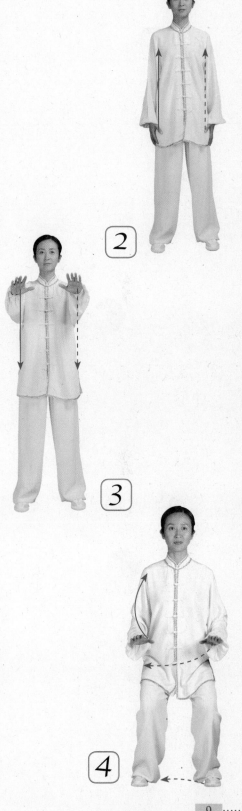

第二式　左右野马分鬃

Form 2　Part the Wild Horse's Mane
(Left- Right-Left Style)

左野马分鬃
Part the Wild Horse's Mane (Left Style)

5 上体微向右转，重心移至右腿上；右臂屈抱于右胸前，手心向下；左臂屈抱于腹前，手心向上，两手心相对成抱球状；左脚随之收至右脚内侧，脚尖点地；眼看右手。

6 上体左转，左脚向左前方迈出一步，脚跟轻轻着地。

7 上体继续左转，重心前移；左腿屈膝前弓，右腿自然蹬直，右脚跟外展，成左弓步；同时两手分别向左上右下分开，左手高与眼平，手心斜向上，肘微屈；右手按至右胯旁，手心向下，指尖向前；眼看左手。

❷ Turn the torso slightly to right and shift weight onto the right leg;bend the right arm horizontally to the front of the right chest,with heart of hand facing downward;move the left arm to the front of abdomen,heart of hand facing upward as if holding a ball with hearts of hands;take the left foot to the inner side of the right foot,the tiptoes of left foot slightly touching the ground.Eyes on right hand.(Fig.5)

❷ Turn the torso to left,left foot takes a step forward to left,with the heel slightly landing on the ground.(Fig.6)

❷ The torso goes on turning to left,shift weight forward and bend the left knee to bow forward,while straighten naturally right leg,turn right heel outward to form a left bow step;at the same time,separate left hand upward and right hand downward, with heart of left hand facing obliquely upward at eye level,with elbow slightly bent;press right hand to side of right hip, with heart of hand facing downward and fingertips pointing forward. Eyes on left hand.(Fig.7)

右野马分鬃
Part the Wild Horse's Mane(Right Style)

8 重心微向后移，左脚尖翘起外撇，眼看左手。

9 上体继续左转，重心移至左腿；同时，右臂逐渐由下往上、由右往左屈至腹前，手心向上；左臂屈至胸前，手心向下，两手上下相对成抱球状；重心移至左腿，左脚踏实，右脚随之收至左脚内侧，脚尖点地；眼看左手。

10 上体微向右转；右脚向右前方迈出一步，脚跟轻轻着地。

11 上体继续右转，重心前移，右脚踏实，右腿屈膝前弓，左腿自然蹬直，成右弓步；同时，两手左下右上分开，右手高与眼平，肘微屈，手心斜向上；左手按至左胯旁，手心向下，指尖向前；眼看右手。

❷ Shift weight slightly backward,raise the tiptoes of left foot to turn outward.Eyes on left hand.(Fig.8)

❷ The torso goes on turning to left;shift weight onto left leg;at the same time,the right arm is gradually bent from bottom to top and from right to left and then to front of abdomen with heart of hand facing upward;left arm is bent to chest with heart of hand facing downward,to form a hold-ball gesture;shift weight onto left leg and set left foot on the ground firmly, withdraw the right foot to the inner side of the left foot,the tiptoes of right foot slightly touching the ground.Eyes on left hand.(Fig.9)

❷ Turn the torso slightly to right;take right foot a step forward to right,with heel slightly landing on the floor. (Fig.10)

❷ The torso goes on turning to right,shift weight forward, set right foot on the ground firmly,bend the right knee to bow forward,while straighten naturally left leg to form a right bow step;at the same time,separate left hand downward and right hand upward,right hand as high as eye level,right elbow bent slightly,hart of right hand facing obliquely upward;while press left hand to side of left hip,with heart of hand facing downward,fingertips pointing forward.Eyes on right hand.(Fig.11)

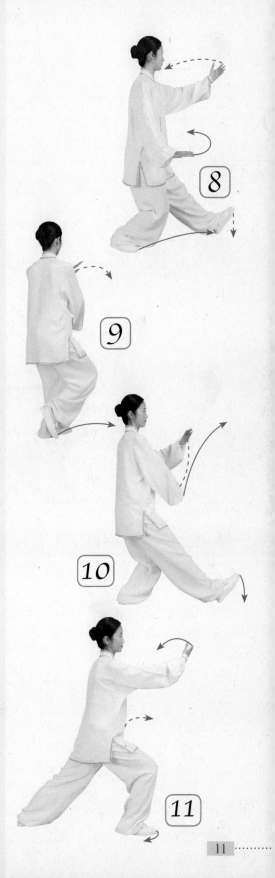

左野马分鬃
Part the Wild Horse's Mane (Left Style)

12 重心稍后移，右脚尖翘起外撇，上体稍右转。

13 ~15，上体继续右转，重心移至右腿。其余动作同左野马分鬃5~7。

❷ Shift weight slightly to backward,raise the tiptoes of right foot to turn outward,turn the torso slightly to right. (Fig.12)

❷ The torso goes on turning to right,shift weight onto the right leg,the other is same as"Part the Wild Horse's Mane"Figs.5~7(Left Style).(Figs.13~15)

要 点

上体不可前俯后仰，胸部必须宽松舒展。两臂分开时要保持弧形。身体转动要以腰为轴。弓步动作与分手的速度要均匀一致。做弓步时，迈出的脚先脚跟着地，然后脚掌慢慢踏实，脚尖向前，膝盖不要超过脚尖；后腿自然伸直；前后脚夹角约45°～60°。野马分鬃式的弓步，前后脚的脚跟要分在中轴线两侧，它们之间的横向距离应保持在10～30厘米左右（即以动作行进中的中线为纵轴，其两侧的垂直距离为横向），以便衔接好下一步动作。

Points to Remember

The torso does not lean forward or backward,and chest must be fully relaxed.Arms should remain rounded when separated. Body turns with lumbar section as the axis.The bow step and parting of hands should go together at an even pace.When to make a bow step,heel taken forward lands on the ground first;and then gradually sets firmly on the ground;knees could not go beyond toes;rear leg straightens naturally;to form angle of 45°～60° between the leg on the ground.Former heel with latter heel stand between straight line,the transverse distance between feet is 10～30cm(Due front of body as vertical axis,both sides of body as a transverse),which is suitable to following forms.

第三式　白鹤亮翅
Form 3　White Crane Spreads Its Wings

16 上体微向左转，右脚向前跟半步；同时，两手翻转相对，在胸前两手相对形成抱球状；左手在上，手心向下；右手在下，手心向上；眼看左手。

17 重心后移，右脚踏实；两手右上左下分开；眼看右手。

18 上体转正；左脚稍向前移动，前脚掌着地，成左虚步；同时右手上提至右额前，手心向左后方；左手按至左胯旁，手心向下，指尖向前；两眼平视前方。

☯ Turn the torso slightly to left,take the right foot half a step forward to the back of the left foot;at the same time,turn the both hands over to face each other to form a hold-ball gesture in front of chest;the left hand is up,with heart of hand facing downward;right hand is down,with heart of hand facing upward.Eyes on left hand.(Fig.16)

☯ Shift weight backward and set right foot on the ground firmly;separate right hand upward and left hand downward.Eyes on right hand.(Fig.17)

☯ Turn the torso to the front;move the left foot forward slightly with the ball of left foot coming down on the ground forming a left empty step;at the same time,raise right hand to front of right forehead,heart of hand facing backward to left; press left hand to side of left hip,with heart of hand facing downward,fingertips pointing forward.Eyes looking straight forward.(Figs.18A,18B)

要 点

胸部不要挺出，两臂要保持半圆形，左膝要微屈，身体重心后移和右手上提、左手下按要协调一致。

Points to Remember

Do not thrust out chest,keep both arms semi-circle,and left knee slightly bent.The shifting back of weight,raising up right hand and pressing down left hand should be coordinated.

第二组
Series Two

[19]

[20]

第四式　左右搂膝拗步
Form 4　Brush Knee and Twist Step
(Left-Right-Left Style)

左搂膝拗步
Brush Knee and Twist Step(Left Style)

19 上体稍左转，右手摆至体前，手心转向上；眼看右手。

20 右手从体前下落，左手由下向上抬升；上体右转，右手向右后方划弧至耳高，手心斜向上；左手向右划弧至右胸前，手心斜向下；左脚收至右脚内侧，脚尖点地；眼看右手。

❷ Turn the torso slightly to left,while right hand swings to front of the body and turn the heart of hand upward. Eyes on right hand.(Fig.19)

❷ Right hand drops downward from the front of body,while left hand raises up from bottom to top;turn the torso to right,right hand moves in a rear-right arc at ear level,with heart of hand facing obliquely upward;left hand moves in a rightward curve to front of right chest,heart of hand facing obliquely downward; withdraw left foot to the inner of the right foot with the tiptoes slightly touching the ground.Eyes on right hand. (Fig.20)

21 上体左转；左脚向左前方迈出一步，脚跟轻轻落地；右臂屈肘，右手与耳同高，手心斜向前；左手下落至腹前，手心向下；眼看前方。

22 上体继续左转；重心前移，左腿屈弓，右腿自然蹬直，成左弓步；同时右手由耳侧向前推出，指尖与鼻尖相对；左手搂过左膝，按至左胯旁，手心向下，指尖向前；眼看右手。

☯ Turn the torso to left;left foot takes a step forward, with the heel slightly landing on the ground;bend right elbow with hand to right ear level,heart of hand facing obliquely forward; left hand drops to front of abdomen,with heart of hand facing downward.Eyes front.(Fig.21)

☯ The torso goes on turning to left;shift weight forward and bend the left knee ,while straighten naturally right leg to form a left bow step;at the same time,right hand pushes out beside ear,fingertips against tip of nose;left hand brushes over left knee,presses beside left hip with heart of hand facing downward, fingertips pointing forward.Eyes on right hand.(Fig.22)

右搂膝拗步
Brush Knee and Twist Step(Right Style)

23 重心稍后移，左脚尖翘起外撇；上体稍向左转，同时右手斜向左，左手斜向右；眼看右手。

☯ Shift weight slightly backward,raise the tiptoes of left foot to turn to the outer side;the torso turns slightly leftward, at the same time,right hand facing obliquely leftward and left hand facing obliquely rightward.Eyes on right hand.(Fig.23)

24 上体继续左转；重心前移，左脚踏实，右脚收至左脚内侧，脚尖点地；左手向左上方划弧至左肩外侧与耳同高，手心斜向上，肘部微屈；右手经体前划弧至左胸前，手心斜向下；眼看左手。

25 上体稍右转；右脚向前迈出一步，脚跟轻轻着地；左手收至左耳侧，手心斜向前；同时右手下落至腹前，手心向下；头转看前方。

26 上体继续右转，重心前移，右腿屈弓，左腿自然蹬直，成右弓步；与此同时右手搂过右膝，按至右胯旁，手心向下，指尖向前；左手向前推出，指尖与鼻尖相对，手心向前，指尖向上；眼看左手。

◐ The torso goes on turning to left;shift weight forward and set left foot firmly on the ground,withdraw the right foot beside the left foot,tiptoes touching the ground;turn left hand upward to left in an arc to outside of left shoulder at ear level,heart of hand facing obliquely upward,elbow slightly bent;right hand moves past the front of body to front of left chest in an arc,heart of hand facing obliquely downward. Eyes on left hand.(Fig.24)

◐ Turn the torso slightly to right;right foot takes a step forward,with the heel slightly landing on the ground;withdraw left hand beside the left ear,with heart of hand facing obliquely forward;at the same time,right hand drops to front of abdomen,with heart of hand facing downward.Turning head to look forward.(Fig.25)

◐ The torso goes on turning to right ,shift weight forward and bend the right leg at knee while straighten naturally left leg to form a right bow step;while right hand brushes over right knee to press beside right hip,with heart of hand facing downward,fingertips pointing forward;left hand pushes forward, fingertips against tip of nose,heart of hand facing forward and fingertips pointing upward. Eyes on left hand.(Fig.26)

左搂膝拗步
Brush Knee and Twist Step(Left Style)

27 重心稍后移，右脚尖翘起外撇，上体右转；两臂外旋；眼看左手。

28 ~30，上体继续右转，重心前移，右脚踏实，左脚收至右脚内侧，脚尖点地；左手划弧至右胸前，手心斜向下；右手向右划弧与耳同高，手心斜向上，右臂自然伸直，肘部微屈；头转看右手。余同20~22。

☯ Shift weight slightly backward,raise the tiptoes of right foot to turn outward,the torso turns to right;turns both arms outward.Eyes on left hand.(Fig.27)

☯ The torso goes on turning to right,shift weight forward and set right foot firmly on the ground,withdraw the left foot beside the right foot,tiptoes touching the ground;move left hand in an arc to front of right chest,with heart of hand facing obliquely downward;and move right hand in an arc to ear level, with heart of hand facing obliquely upward,right arm stretches naturally,with elbow slightly bent.Turning head to look at right hand.(Figs.28~30) The other is same as Figs.20~22 (Left Style).

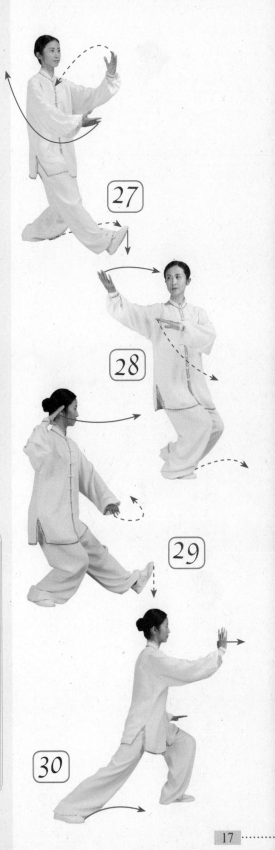

27

28

29

30

要 点

　　前掌推出时，身体不可前俯后仰，要松腰松胯。推掌时要沉肩垂肘，坐腕舒掌，同时须与松腰、弓腿上下协调一致。搂膝拗步成弓步时，两脚跟的横向距离保持约30厘米左右。

Points to Remember

When palm pushes out,the torso does not lean forward or backward,waist and hips should be relaxed.In pushing out palm,lower shoulder and loosen elbow,keeping wrist sat and fingers unfolded with ease would be coordinated with relaxation of waist and bending of leg.When forming a bow step,transverse distance between heels is about 30cm.

第五式 手挥琵琶

Form 5 Hand Strums the Lute（Pipa）

31 右脚向前跟半步，脚尖轻落于左脚后；右臂稍向前伸，腕关节放松。

32 重心后移，右脚踏实，上体右转；左手向左、向上划弧至体前，手臂自然伸直，手心斜向下；右手收至胸前，手心斜向下；眼转看左手。

33 上体稍向左转，左脚跟着地，成左虚步；同时左手向上挑举，右手回收，屈肘合抱；左手与鼻尖同高，手心向右；右手与左肘相对，手心向左；眼看左手。

☯ Right foot takes half a step forward,with tiptoes touching slightly the ground after the left foot;right arm streches slightly forward with the wrist relaxed.(Fig.31)

☯ Shift weight backward,and then set right foot on the ground firmly,the torso turns to right;raise the left hand in a leftward-upward arc to front of body,stretching naturally the arm,with heart of hand facing obliquely downward;right hand draw back to front of chest,with heart of hand facing obliquely downward.Eyes turning on left hand.(Fig.32)

☯ The torso turns slightly to left,with the left heel landing on the ground to form a left empty step;at the same time,raise and snap left hand upward,while right hand withdraws back,bent to close; left hand level is the same as tip of nose,heart of hand facing rightward;right hand is against left elbow,heart of hand facing leftward.Eyes on left hand.(Fig.33)

要　点

　　身体要平稳自然，沉肩垂肘，胸部放松。左手上起时不要直向上挑，要由左向上、向前，微带弧形。右脚跟进时，前脚掌先着地，再全脚落实。

Points to Remember

Body position should remain steady and natural.Lower shoulders and loosen elbows with chest relaxed. In coming up, left hand should not come up straight,but in a curve upward from left,and then forward.In stepping forward with right foot,ball of it touches on the ground first and then sets sole firm on the ground.

第六式　左右倒卷肱

Form 6　Step Back and Whirl Arms
(Right-Left-Right-Left Style)

右倒卷肱
Step Back and Whirl Arms(Right Style)

34 上体稍右转；两手翻转向上；右手向下经腰侧向后上方划弧，右臂微屈，手与头同高；左手翻转于体前；眼看右手。

35 上体稍左转；左脚提收向后退一步，脚前掌轻轻落地；右臂屈肘，右手收至右耳侧，手心斜向下；左手开始后收；眼看左手。

36 上体继续左转，重心后移，左脚踏实，右脚以脚掌为轴扭正，脚跟离地，右膝微屈成右虚步；右手经右耳侧推至体前，腕与肩同高，手心向前；左手向后、向下划弧，收至左肋外侧，手心向上；眼看右手。

❂ Turn the torso slightly to right;both hands turn over upward;right hand moves downward past the side of the waist to upper rear in an arc,with right arm slightly bent;the hand is the same as head level;left hand is turned before the body.Eyes on right hand.(Fig.34)

❂ The torso turns slightly to left;withdraw and raise left foot to take a step backward,the ball of left foot coming down gently on the ground;bend the elbow of right arm,right hand comes to side of ear level,with heart of hand facing obliquely downward;the left hand is going to withdraw backward.Eyes on left hand.(Fig.35)

❂ The torso goes on turning to left,shift weight backward and set left foot on the ground firmly,the right foot is turned straight,using the ball of the foot as pivot,the heel off the ground,while the right knee is bent slightly to form right empty step;the right hand past the side of right ear pushes to front of body,the wrist is as high as shoulder,heart of hand facing forward;left hand moves in a backward-downward arc,and withdraw to outer side of left ribs,heart of hand facing upward. Eyes on right hand.(Fig.36)

左倒卷肱
Step Back and Whirl Arms (Left Style)

37 上体稍左转；左手向左后上方划弧，与头同高，手心向上，左臂微屈；右手翻转于体前，手心向上；眼看左手。

38 上体稍右转，右脚提收向后退一步，脚前掌轻轻落地；左臂屈肘，左手收至左耳侧，手心斜向下；右手开始后收；眼看右手。

39 上体继续右转；重心后移，右脚踏实，左脚以脚掌为轴扭正，脚跟离地，左膝微屈成左虚步；左手经左耳侧推至体前，腕与肩同高，手心向前；右手向后、向下划弧，收至右肋外侧，手心向上；眼看左手。

☯ The torso turns slightly to left;left hand comes up behind to upper in an arc to the level of the head,heart of hand facing upward,the arm is slightly bent;the right hand is turned to front of body,heart of hand facing upward.Eyes on left hand.(Fig.37)

☯ The torso turns slightly to right,draw and raise right foot to take a step backward,the ball of the foot comes down gently on the ground;bent left arm at elbow,the hand is withdrawn to side of left ear,with heart of hand facing obliquely downward; the right hand is going to withdraw backward.Eyes on right hand.(Fig.38)

☯ The torso goes on turning to right;shift weight backward and set right foot on the ground firmly,the left foot is turned straight,using the ball of the foot as pivot,with the heel off the ground,while the left knee is bent slightly to form left empty step; pushes the left hand past the side of left ear to front of body,the wrist is at shoulder level,heart of hand facing forward;right hand moves in a backward-downward arc,and withdraw it to outer side of right ribs,heart of hand facing upward.Eyes on left hand.(Fig.39)

右倒卷肱
Step Back and Whirl Arms (Right Style)

40

~42，重复34~36的动作。

☯ repeat the actions of "Step Back and Whirl Arms(Right Style)"as Figs.34~36.(Figs.40~42)

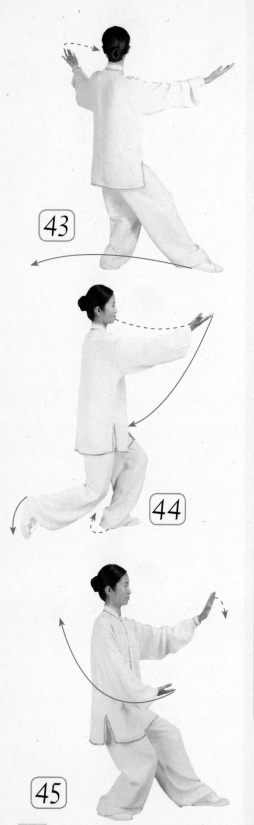

左倒卷肱
Step Back and Whirl Arms (Left Style)

43 ~45，重复37~39的动作。

✪ repeat the actions of "Step Back and Whirl Arms(Left Style)"as Figs.37~39.(Figs.43~45)

要　点

前推的手不要伸直，后撤的手也不可直向回抽，随转体仍走弧线。前推时，要转腰松胯，两手的速度要一致，避免僵硬。退步时，脚掌先着地，再慢慢全脚踏实；同时前脚随转体以脚掌为轴扭正。退左脚略向左后斜，退右脚略向右后斜，避免使两脚落在一条直线上。后退时，眼神随转体动作先向左右看，然后再转看前手。

Points to Remember

The hand pushing forward should not be streched straight,the withdrawing hand should not be withdrawn straight back,but in a curve.In pushing forward,turn at waist with hips relaxed and both hands moving at an even pace,avoiding stiffness.In retreat,land on ball of foot first,gradually setting the sole firmly on the ground,while the foot in front turns naturally straight at the ball as pivot.The retreating left foot should turn obliquely towards rear-left,the retreating right obliquely towards rear-right.And avoid both feet to drop on one straight line.In retreating movement,following the turn of torso,eyes on either side,and then on front hand.

第七式　左揽雀尾

Form 7　Grasp the Bird's Tail(Left Style)

46 上体微右转；右手由肋旁向右上方划弧，右臂微屈，手与肩同高，手心斜向上；左手在体前放松，手心向下；眼向右平视。

47 右臂平屈至右胸前，手心转向下；左手划弧下落，屈抱于腹前，手心转向上，两手相对成抱球状；左脚收至右脚内侧，脚尖点地；眼看右手。

48 上体微左转，左脚向左前方迈出一步，脚跟轻轻落地；眼看前方。

❀ Turn the torso slightly to right;the right hand moves past the side of right ribs in an upper-right arc,right arm is slightly bent,the hand is the same as shoulder level,heart of hand facing obliqiely upward;while keep left hand relaxed before the body,heart of hand facing downward.Eyes looking straight to right.(Fig.46)

❀ Right arm is horizontally bent to front of right chest, heart of hand turned downward;while left hand drops down in a curve,close to front of abdomen,heart of hand turned upward, both hands to form a hold-ball gesture;withdraw the left foot to the inner side of the right foot,tiptoes touching the ground. Eyes on right hand.(Fig.47)

❀ The torso turns slight to left,left foot takes a step forward to left,with the heel landing on the ground gently. Eyes front.(Fig.48)

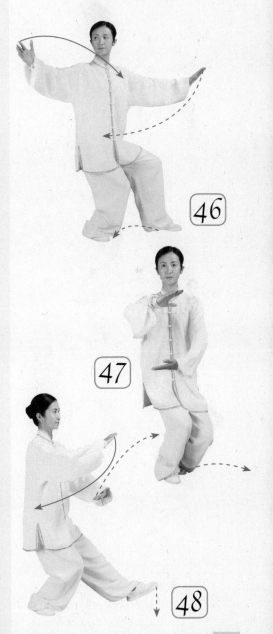

49 上体继续左转；重心前移，左脚踏实，左腿屈膝前弓，右腿自然蹬直成左弓步；同时两手前后分开，左臂向前向上掤出，腕与肩同高，手心向内；右手向下划弧按于右胯旁，手心向下，指尖向前；眼看左手。

50 上体微左转，左手向左前方伸出，手心转向下；同时右手经腹前向上、向前伸至左前臂内侧，手心向上；眼看左手。

51 上体右转，两臂同时向下经腹前向右后方划弧后捋，右手举于身体侧后方，与头同高，手心斜向外；左臂平屈于胸前，手心向内；重心后移，身体后坐，右腿屈膝，左腿自然伸直；眼看右手。

52 上体左转，正对前方；右臂屈肘，右手搭于左腕内侧，手心向前；左前臂仍屈收于胸前，手心向内，指尖向右；眼看前方。

❧ The torso goes on turning to left;shift weight forward and set left foot firmly on the ground,left leg is bent at knee to bow forward, while straighten naturally right leg to form a left bow step;at the same time,separate both hands to front and back,left arm thrusts forward and upward with wrist at shoulder level,heart of hand facing inward;right hand presses downward in a curve to side of right hip,heart of hand facing downward, with fingertips pointing forward.Eyes on left hand.(Fig.49)

❧ The torso turns to left a little,left hand extends forward to left,heart of hand turned downward;while right hand extends past abdomen upward and forward to inner side of left forearm, heart of hand facing upward.Eyes on left hand.(Fig.50)

❧ Turn the torso to right,while stroke both arms down past abdomen to rear-right in an arc,until right hand raises up to side-rear of body,at head level,heart of hand facing obliquely outward;left arm is bent horizontally to front of the chest, heart of hand turned inward;shift weight backward,sit back onto right leg,which is bent at knee,while stretch left leg naturally. Eyes on right hand.(Fig.51)

❧ Turn the torso to left and due face the front;right arm is bent at elbow,with right hand close to inside of left wrist, heart of hand facing forward;left forearm is still bent to front of the chest,heart of hand facing inward,fingertips pointing rightward.Eyes front.(Fig.52)

53 重心前移，左腿屈弓，右腿自然蹬直成左弓步；与此同时，双手向前慢慢挤出，与肩同高，两臂撑圆；眼看前方。

54 左手翻转向下，右手经左腕上方向前伸出，手心翻转向下；两手左右分开，与肩同宽；眼向前平视。

55 重心后移，上体后坐，右腿屈膝，左腿自然伸直，左脚尖翘起；两臂屈收后引，经胸前收到腹前，手心斜向下；眼向前平视。

56 重心前移，左脚踏实，左腿屈弓，右腿自然蹬直成左弓步；两手向前、向上推按至体前，两腕与肩同高、同宽，两手心向前，指尖向上；眼平看前方。

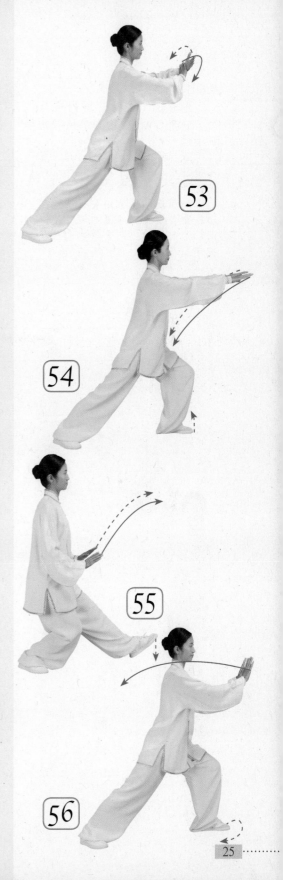

❂ Shift weight forward and bend the left leg at knee to bow forward,while straighten naturally right leg to form a left bow step;at the same time,press both hands slowly forward at shoulder level,both arms rounded.Eyes front.(Fig.53)

❂ Turn left hand downward,right hand passes over left wrist and moves forward,turn heart of hand downward;separate both hands to the side of the left and the right,they are shoulder-width apart.Eyes looking straight forward.(Fig.54)

❂ Shift weight backward and sit back onto right leg,which is bent at knee,while stretch left leg naturally,raise the tiptoes of left foot;withdraw both arms back past the front of the chest to front of abdomen,hearts of hands facing obliquely downward. Eyes looking straight forward. (Fig.55)

❂ Shift weight forward,set left foot firmly on the ground, left leg is bent at knee to bow,while straighten right leg naturally to form a left bow step;push both hands forward and upward to front of body,both wrists at shoulder level and shoulder-width apart,hearts of hands facing forward with fingertips pointing upward.Eyes looking straight forward. (Fig.56)

要 点

棚出时，两臂前后均保持弧形，分掌与松腰、弓腿三者必须协调一致。

下掯时，上体不可前倾，臀部不要凸出。两臂下掯须随腰旋转，仍走弧线。左脚全掌着地。

向前挤时，上体要正直。挤的动作要与松腰、弓腿协调一致。

向前按时，两手须走曲线，手腕部高与肩平，两肘微屈。

Points to Remember

When thrusting forward,keep both arms arc.The separation of palms,relaxtion of waist and bending of leg must be coordinated.
When stroking arms down,the torso does not lean forward,and does not jut buttocks out while stroking both arms down,they should follow the moving of the waist, still in a line of arc. The sole of the left foot sets fully on the ground.
When pressing forward,keep body erect.Coordinate pressing with relaxation of the waist and bending of the legs.
When pushing forward,both hands are moved in a curve and wrists are at the level of shoulder with both elbows slightly bending.

第八式　右揽雀尾
Form 8　Grasp the Bird's Tail(Right Style)

57 重心后移，上体右转，左脚尖内扣；右手向右侧划弧，左手伸展于左侧，两肘稍垂，两手心均向外；眼看右手。

58 重心左移，左腿屈膝，右脚收至左脚内侧，脚尖点地；左手屈抱于左胸前，手心向下；右手屈抱于腹前，手心向上，两手相对形成抱球状；眼看左手。

59 上体微右转，右脚向右前方迈出一步，脚跟轻轻落地；眼看前方。

❸ Shift weight backward,turn the torso to right,tiptoes of left foot turned inward;right hand moves to right side in an arc,and left hand is extended to left side,both elbows lowering slightly,hearts of hands completely outward. Eyes on right hand. (Fig.57)

❸ Shift weight to left,left leg is bent at knee,withdraw the right foot to the inner side of the left foot,with tiptoes touching the ground;bend left hand to front of left chest,heart of hand facing downward;right hand to front of the abdomen, heart of hand facing upward,to form a hold-ball gesture.Eyes on left hand.(Fig.58)

❸ The torso turns slightly to right,right foot takes a step forward to right,with the heel landing on the ground gently. Eyes front.(Fig.59)

60上体继续右转，重心前移，右脚踏实，右腿屈膝前弓，左腿自然蹬直，成右弓步；两手前后分开，右臂向前向上掤出，腕与肩同高，手心向内；左手向下划弧按至左胯旁，手心向下，指尖向前；眼看右手。

61上体稍右转；右手向右前方伸出，手心转向下；同时，左手经腹前向上、向前伸至右前臂内侧，手心向上；眼看右手。

62上体左转；两臂同时向下经腹前向左后方划弧后捋，左手举于身体侧后方，与头同高，手心斜向外；右臂平屈于胸前，手心向内；重心后移，身体后坐，左腿屈膝，右腿自然伸直；眼看左手。

63上体右转，正对前方；左臂屈肘，左手搭于右腕内侧，手心向前；右前臂仍屈于胸前，手心向内，指尖向左；眼看前方。

☻ The torso goes on turning to right,shift weight forward and set right foot firmly on the ground,right leg is bent at knee to bow forward,left leg straightens naturally to form a right bow step;while separate both hands to front and back,right arm thrusts forward,wrist at shoulder level,heart of hand facing inward;left hand presses down to side of left hip in an arc, heart of hand facing downward,fingertips pointing forward.Eyes on right hand.(Fig.60)

☻ The torso turns to right a little;right hand extends to front-right,heart of hand turned downward;at the same time, left hand extends past front of abdomen upward-forward to inner side of right forearm,heart of hand facing upward.Eyes on right hand.(Fig.61)

☻ Turn the torso to left;while stroke both arms down past the front of abdomen to rear-left in an arc,until left hand reaches to side rear of body,at head level,heart of hand facing obliquely outward right arm is bent horizontally to front of the chest,heart of hand turned inward;shift weight backward, sit back onto left leg,which is bent at knee,while stretch right leg naturally.Eyes on left hand.(Fig.62)

☻ Turn the torso to right and due face the front;left arm bent at elbow,with left hand closes to inside of right wrist,heart of hand facing forward,right forearm still bent before the chest,heart of hand facing inward,fingertips pointing leftward. Eyes front.(Fig.63)

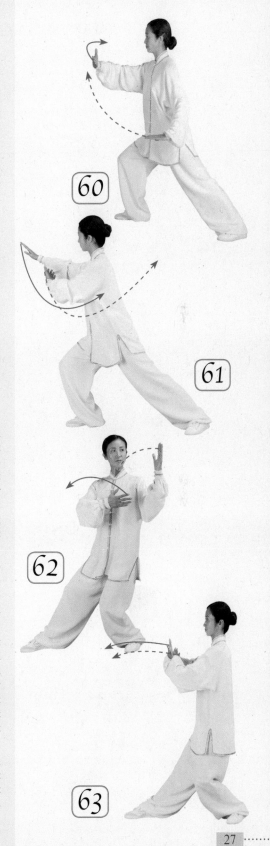

60

61

62

63

64 重心前移，右腿屈弓，左腿自然蹬直成右弓步；与此同时，双手慢慢向体前挤出，与肩同高，两臂撑圆；眼看前方。

65 重心后移，上体后坐，左腿屈膝，右腿自然伸直，右脚尖翘起；右手翻转向下，左手经右腕上方向前伸出，手心转向下；两手左右分开，与肩同宽，两臂屈收后引，经胸前收到腹前，手心斜向下；眼向前平视。

66 重心前移，右脚踏实，右腿屈弓，左腿自然蹬直成右弓步；两手向前、向上推按至体前，两腕与肩同高、同宽，两手心向前，指尖向上；眼平视前方。

◐ Shift weight forward and bend the right leg at knee while straighten naturally left leg to form a right bow step;at the same time,press both hands slowly forward at shoulder level, both arms are rounded.Eyes front.(Fig.64)

◐ Shift weight backward and sit back onto left leg,which is bent at knee,while stretch right leg naturally,raises the tiptoes of right foot;right hand turned downward,left hand passes over right wrist and moves forward,heart of hand turned downward;both hands are separated to the side of the left and the right,shoulder width-apart,withdraw both arms back past front of chest down to front of the abdomen,hearts of hands facing obliquely downward. Eyes looking straight forward. (Fig.65)

◐ Shift weight forward,set right foot firmly on the ground, right leg is bent to bow,while straighten left leg naturally to form a right bow step;push both hands upward and forward to front of body,wrists at shoulder level and shoulder-width apart,hearts of hands facing forward with fingertips pointing upward.Eyes looking straight forward.(Fig.66)

要 点

均与左揽雀尾相同，惟左右相反。

Points to Remember

"Grasp the Bird's Tail(Right Style)" is the same as Form 7 ,only with left and right reversed.

第九式　单鞭

Form 9　Single Whip

67 上体左转，重心移至左腿，右脚尖内扣；左手经面前向左划弧至身体左侧，手心向外；右手经腹前向左划弧至左肋前，手心斜向内；眼看左手。

68 上体右转，重心右移，右腿屈膝；左手向下、向右划弧至腹前；右手向上、向右划弧至肩高，手心向外；眼看右手。

69 左脚收至右脚内侧，脚尖点地；右手翻转向下变成勾手，腕与肩平；左手向上、向右划弧至右肩前，手心转向内；眼看勾手。

❍ Turn the torso to left ,shift weight onto left leg,with tiptoes of right foot turned inward;left hand moves past the front of face in leftward arc to the side of body,heart of hand facing outward;right hand moves past the front of abdomen in leftward arc to front of left ribs,heart of hand facing obliquely inward.Eyes on left hand.(Fig.67)

❍ Turn the torso to right,shift weight onto right leg while bend right leg at knee;left hand moves in a downward and rightward arc to front of abdomen;right hand moves in an upward and rightward arc to shoulder level,heart of hand facing outward.Eyes on right hand.(Fig.68)

❍ Withdraw the left foot to the inner side of right foot,the tiptoes touching the ground;right hand is turned downward to form a hooked hand,wrist at shoulder level;left hand moves upward-rightward arc to front of right shoulder,with heart of hand is turned inward.Eyes on hooked hand.(Fig.69)

70 上体稍左转；左脚向左前方迈出一步，脚跟着地，左手向左划弧，手心向内；眼看左手。

第四组
Series Four

67

68

69

71 上体继续左转，重心前移，左脚踏实，左腿屈弓，右腿自然蹬直，脚跟外展，成斜向左前方的弓步；左手经面前翻转向前推出，手心向前，手指与眼同高，臂微屈，左肘与左膝上下相对；眼看左手。

● The torso turns slightly to left;left foot takes a step forward to left,the heel landing on the ground,left hand moves leftward in an arc,heart of hand facing inward. Eyes on left hand. (Fig.70)

● The torso goes on turning to left,shift weight forward,set left foot firmly on the ground,left leg is bent to bow,while straighten right leg naturally,right heel outward,to form a left bow step which is forward obliquely to left;left hand turned pushes out past the front of face,heart of hand facing forward,fingers at eyes level,the arm is bent slightly,left elbow is in vertical line with left knee.Eyes on left hand.(Fig.71)

要 点

　　上体正直，松腰。右臂肘部稍下垂，左肘与左膝上下相对，两肩下沉。左手向外翻掌前推时，要随转体边翻边推出，不要翻掌太快或最后突然翻掌。全部过渡动作，上下要协调一致。

Points to Remember

Keep torso erect and waist relaxed.Right elbows is bent down a bit,and left elbow is in vertical line with left knee,with both shoulders lowered.When pushing out,left palm turns out gradually with the movement of torso,and not too fast or abruptly.In all the transitional movements,the upper and lower halves of body must be well coordinated.

第十式　云手
Form 10　Wave Hands Like Clouds on Both Sides

72 重心后移，上体右转，左脚尖内扣，右腿屈弓；左手向右上划弧，经腹前至右肩前，手心向内；右勾手松开变掌，手心向外；眼看右手。

● Shift weight backward,the torso turns to right,tiptoes of left foot turned inward,while bend right leg to bow;left hand moves in an upper-right arc,past the front of abdomen to the front of right shoulder,heart of hand is turned inward;turn the right hooked hand into palm,heart of hand facing outward.Eyes on right hand.(Fig.72)

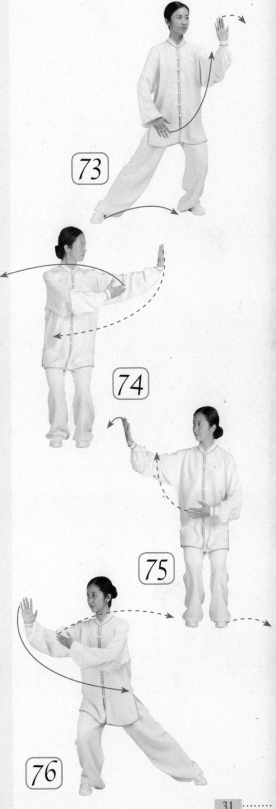

73 上体左转，重心移至左腿；右手向下划弧至腹前，手心向内；左手向上划弧至左肩前，腕与肩高，手心斜向内；眼看左手。

74 右脚向左脚平行并拢，脚前掌先着地，随之全脚踏实，两腿屈膝半蹲，脚尖向前，两脚相距约10厘米。左手向左划弧，手心渐渐翻转向外；同时右手由腹前向左划弧至左肩前，手心渐渐翻转向内；眼看左手。

75 上体右转，重心移至右腿；右手经头前向右划弧，右腕与右肩同高，手心斜向内；左手向下划弧至腹前，手心向内；眼看右手。

76 左脚向左横开一步，脚前掌先着地，随之全脚踏实，脚尖向前；右手逐渐翻转向外，左手向上划弧至右肩前，手心逐渐翻转向内；眼看右手。

❂ The torso turns to left,shift weight onto left leg;right hand moves a down arc to front of abdomen,heart of hand facing inward;left hand moves an upward arc to the front of left shoulder,wrist at shoulder level,heart of hand facing obliquely inward.Eyes on left hand.(Fig.73)

❂ Bring right foot at parallel to within about 10cm of left foot,the ball of right foot lands first on the ground,and then sitting firmly on right foot,both knees bent to half squat, tiptoes pointing forward.Left hand moves to left in an arc, heart of hand turned gradually outward;at the same time,right hand moves past the front of abdomen in a leftward arc to front of left shoulder,heart of hand turned gradually obliquely inward.Eyes on left hand.(Fig.74)

❂ The torso turns to right,shift weight onto right leg;right hand moves past the front of head in rightward arc,right wrist at right shoulder level,with heart of hand facing obliquely inward;left hand moves downward arc to front of abdomen,with heart of hand facing inward.Eyes on right hand.(Fig.75)

❂ Left foot takes left a side step,the ball of left foot lands first on the ground,and then sit firmly on left foot,with tiptoes pointing forward;right hand turns gradually outward, while left hand moves in upward arc to front of right shoulder,heart of hand turned obliquely inward. Eyes on right hand.(Fig.76)

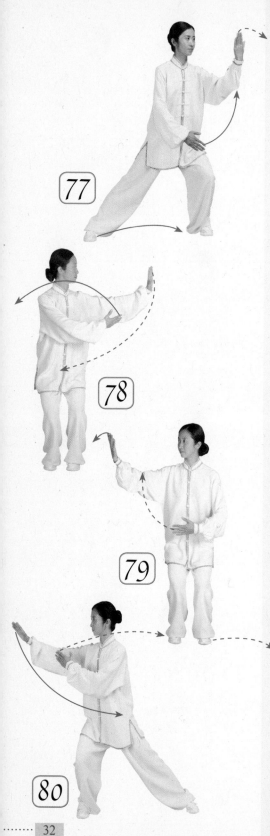

77 上体左转，重心移至左腿；右手向下划弧至腹前，手心渐渐翻转向内；左手经头前向左划弧至左肩前，手心斜向内；眼看左手。

78 右脚向左脚并拢，脚前掌先着地，随之全脚踏实，两脚屈膝半蹲，两脚平行，脚尖向前，两脚相距约10厘米；左手向左划弧至身体左侧，手心渐渐翻转向外，高与肩平；右手继续往左划弧至左肩前，手心渐渐翻转向内；眼看左手。

79 上体右转，重心右移至右腿；右手经头前向右划弧，右腕与右肩同高，手心斜向内，左手向下划弧至腹前，手心向内；眼看右手。

80 左脚向左横开一步，脚前掌着地，随之全脚踏实，脚尖向前；右手划弧至身体右侧，手心逐渐翻转向外，高与肩平；左手向上划弧至右肩前，手心逐渐翻转向内；眼看右手。

☯ Turn the torso to left,shift weight onto left leg;right hand moves in downward arc to front of abdomen,heart of hand turned gradually inward;left hand moves past front of head in leftward arc to left shoulder,heart of hand facing obliquely inward.Eyes on left hand.(Fig.77)

☯ Bring right foot at parallel to within about 10cm of left foot,the ball of right foot lands first on the ground,and then sitting firmly on right foot,both knees bent to half squat, tiptoes pointing forward;left hand moves left in an arc to left side of body,heart of hand turned gradually outward,at shoulder level;right hand continues to moves in a leftward arc to front of left shoulder,heart of hand turned gradually inward.Eyes on left hand.(Fig.78)

☯ The torso turns to right,shift weight onto right leg;right hand moves past the front of head in rightward arc,right wrist at right shoulder level,with heart of hand facing obliquely inward;left hand moves downward arc to front of abdomen,with heart of hand facing inward.Eyes on right hand.(Fig.79)

☯ Left foot takes left a side step,the ball of left foot lands first on the ground,and then sit firmly on left foot,with tiptoes pointing forward;right hand moves in an arc to right side of body,heart of hand turned gradually outward,at shoulder level;left hand moves in upward arc to front of right shoulder,heart of hand turned gradually inward.Eyes on right hand.(Fig.80)

81 上体左转，重心移至左腿；右手向下划弧至腹前，手心渐渐翻转向内，左手经头前向左划弧至左肩前，手心斜向内；眼看左手。

82 右脚向左脚并拢，脚前掌先着地，随之全脚踏实，两脚屈膝半蹲，两脚平行，脚尖向前，两脚相距约10厘米；左手向左划弧至身体左侧，手心渐渐翻转向外，高与肩平；右手继续往左划弧至左肩前，手心渐渐翻转向内；眼看左手。

❻ Turn the torso to left,shift weight onto left leg;right hand moves in downward arc to front of abdomen,heart of right hand turned slowly inward,left hand moves past the front of head in a leftward arc to front of left shoulder,heart of hand facing obliquely inward.Eyes on left hand.(Fig.81)

❻ Bring right foot at parallel to within about 10cm of left foot,the ball of right foot lands first on the ground,and then sitting firmly on right foot,both knees bent to half squat, tiptoes pointing forward;left hand moves left in an arc to left side of body,heart of hand turned gradually outward,at shoulder level;right hand continues to move in a leftward arc to front of left shoulder,heart of hand turned gradually inward.Eyes on left hand.(Fig.82)

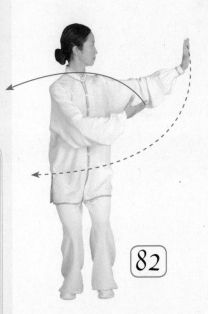

要 点

　　身体转动要以腰脊为轴，松腰，松胯，不可忽高忽低。两臂随腰的转动而运转，要自然圆活，速度要缓慢均匀。下肢移动时，身体重心要稳定。眼的视线随左右手而移动。

Points to Remember

Lumbar spine is the axis for body turns.Keep waist and hips relaxed and avoid sudden ups and downs in stance.Movements of arms should be natural and circular at an even pace,following the waist.When moving lower limbs,keep body steady.Eyes should follow left hand and right hand moving.

第十一式 单鞭

Form 11 Single Whip

83 上体右转，重心移向右腿，右手经头前向右划弧，右腕与右肩同高，手心斜向内；左手向下划弧至腹前，手心向内；眼看右手。

84 当右手划弧至右前方时，翻转变勾手，腕与肩平；左手由腹前划弧至右肩前，手心转向内，提起左脚。眼看勾手。

85 ～86，其余同单鞭70、71。

☯ Turn the torso to right,shift weight onto right leg;right hand moves in a rightward arc past the front of head,right wrist at right shoulder level,heart of hand facing obliquely inward;left hand moves in a downward arc to front of abdomen,heart of hand facing inward.Eyes on right hand. (Fig.83)

☯ When right hand moves an arc to front-right,heart of hand turned over to form a hooked hand,wrist at shoulder level;left hand moves an arc from the front of abdomen to the front of right shoulder,with heart of hand turned inward,raise left foot.Eyes on hooked hand. (Fig.84)

☯ repeat the actions of Form 9"Single Whip"as Figs.70, 71. (Figs.85, 86)

要 点

与第九式单鞭相同。

Points to Remember

It's same as Form 9.

第十二式　高探马

Form 12　High Pat on Horse

87 右脚向前跟半步，脚前掌着地；眼看左手。

88 上体稍右转，重心后移至右腿；同时左脚跟提起，右勾手松开；两手翻转，手心向上；两臂的肘关节微屈；眼看右手。

89 上体稍左转，面对前方，右手经右耳侧向前推出，腕与肩同高，手心向前，左手收至左腹前，手心向上；与此同时，左脚稍前移，脚掌着地，成左虚步；眼看右手。

❧ Right foot takes half a step forward,the ball of right foot lands on the ground.Eyes on left hand.(Fig.87)

❧ The torso turns slightly to right,shift weight backward on to right leg;at the same time,left heel raised,right hooked hand opens into a palm;both hands turn over,hearts of hands facing upward;elbow joints of both arms are bent slightly.Eyes on right hand.(Fig.88)

❧ The torso turns slightly to left,facing forward,right hand moves past the side of right ear to push forward,with wrist at shoulder level,heart of hand facing forward,left hand is withdrawn to front of left abdomen,heart of hand facing upward;meanwhile,left foot moves slightly forward,the ball of left foot lands on the ground,to form a left empty step.Eyes on right hand.(Fig.89)

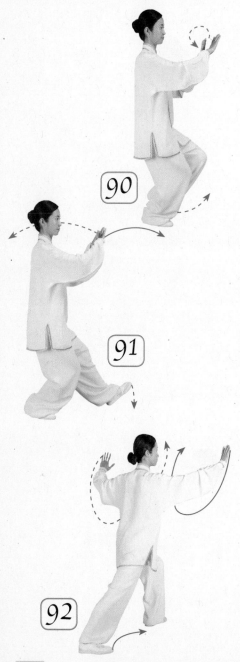

第十三式 右蹬脚
Form 13　Kick with Right Heel

90 左脚收至右脚内侧，左手前伸至右手背穿出，两腕相交；左手心斜向上，右手心斜向下；眼看左手。

91 上体左转；左脚向左前方迈出，脚跟着地；左手内旋，手心皆向外；眼看左手。

92 重心前移，左脚踏实，左腿屈弓，右腿自然蹬直成左弓步；同时两手向左右分开，手心向前；眼看右手。

◐ Withdraw left foot beside right foot,left hand extends forward through over the back of right hand,both wrists crossed;heart of left hand facing obliquely upward,heart of right hand facing obliquely downward.Eyes on left hand. (Fig.90)

◐ The torso turns to left;left foot takes a step forward to left,heel on the ground;left hand turns inward,hearts of hands completely outward.Eyes on left hand.(Fig.91)

◐ Shift weight forward,sit firmly on left foot,bend the left leg at knee ,while straighten right leg naturally to form a left bow step;at the same time,separate both hands to the side of the left and the right,with hearts of hands facing forward.Eyes on right hand.(Fig.92)

93 右脚收至左脚内侧，脚尖点地；两手向腹前划弧相交合抱，举至胸前，右手在外，两手心皆向内；眼看右前方。

94 两手向左右撑开，两臂平举，两腕与肩平，手心向外；与此同时，屈右膝提右腿，用脚跟向右前方蹬出，右臂与右腿上下相对，方向为右前方约30°；眼看右手。

● Withdraw right foot beside left foot,tiptoes on the ground; cross both hands in front of abdomen and up to front of chest,right hand is outer,with hearts of hands completely inward.Eyes toward front-right.(Fig.93)

● Extend both hands to the side of the left and the right,both arms raise horizontally,both wrists at shoulder level,with hearts of hands facing outward;at the same time,bend right knee to lift,kick with the right heel forward to right,right arm is in vertical line with right leg,the direction being about 30°forward to right.Eyes on right hand.(Fig.94)

93

要 点

身体要稳定，不可前俯后仰。两手分开时，腕部与肩平齐。蹬脚时，左腿微屈，右脚尖回勾，劲使在脚跟，分手和蹬脚须协调一致。右臂和右腿上下相对。

Points to Remember

Keep your balance,don't lean forward or backward. When both hands separate,wrists are level with shoulders.When kicking,left leg is bent slightly,tiptoes of right foot should be upturned enough to have the kicking force focus on heel.The separation of hands should be coordinated with the kick.The right arm is in vertical line with the right leg.

94

95

96

97

第十四式　双峰贯耳
Form 14　Strike Opponent's Ears with Both Fists

95 右腿屈膝回收，脚尖自然下垂；左手向体前划弧与右手平行，落于右膝上方，手心皆向上，指尖向前；眼看前方。

96 右脚向右前方落步，脚跟落地，两手收至两腰侧，手心向上；眼看前方。

97 重心前移，右脚踏实，右腿屈弓，左腿自然蹬直，成右弓步；两手握拳从两侧向上、向前划弧摆至头前；两拳相对成钳形，相距同头宽，拳眼斜向下；眼看前方。

❶ Withdraw right leg and bend the knee,with tiptoes pointing naturally downward;left hand moves in an arc to front of body,in parallel with right hand,dropping over right knee,hearts of hands completely upward,,fingertips pointing forward.Eyes front.(Fig.95)

❶ Drop the right foot forward to right,heel on the ground, both hands are withdrawn to both sides of waist,hearts of hands facing upward.Eyes front.(Fig.96)

❶ Shift weight forward,set right foot firmly on the ground,bend right leg at knee to bow while straighten left leg naturally to form a right bow step;both hands gradually clench to fists and then the arms make an arc upward and forward from the both sides of waist to the front of head;both fists make a strike in a pincer movement,fists apart as wide as the head,eyes of fists facing diagonally downwards.Eyes front. (Fig.97)

要　点

　　头颈正直，松腰松胯，两拳松握，沉肩垂肘，两臂均保持弧形。

Points to Remember

Hold head and neck erect,and keep waist and hips relaxed,fists loosely clenched.Shoulders are lowered and elbows hung slightly bent.Keep both arms rounded.

第十五式 转身左蹬脚

Form 15 Turn and Kick with Left Heel

98 重心移至左腿，右脚尖内扣，两拳松开，两手由上向左右划弧分开，手心向外；眼看左手。

99 重心移至右腿，左脚收至右脚内侧，脚尖点地；两手交叉合抱于胸前，左手在外，两手心皆向内；眼看前方。

100 两手向左右撑开，两臂平举，两腕与肩平，手心向外；与此同时，屈左膝提左腿，用脚跟向左前方蹬出，左臂与左腿上下相对，方向为左前方约30°；眼看左手。

❻ Shift weight onto left leg,right tiptoes turns inward,open both fists to palms,making an arc from the upside to left and right,hearts of hands facing outward.Eyes on left hand. (Fig.98)

❻ Shift weight onto right leg,withdraw left foot beside right foot,tiptoes touching on the ground;cross hands in front of the chest,left hand is outer,with hearts of hands completely facing inward.Eyes front.(Fig.99)

❻ Extend both hands to the side of the left and the right,both arms are horizontally raised,both wrists are at shoulder level,with hearts of hands outward;at the same time,raise left leg with bent at knee,kick with the left heel forward to left,left arm is in vertical line with left leg,the direction being front to left about 30°.Eyes on left hand.(Fig.100)

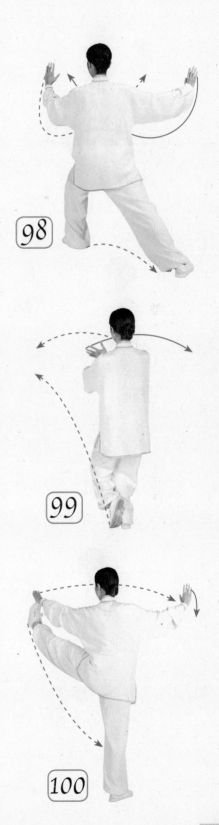

要 点

与右蹬脚式相同，惟左右相反。

Points to Remember

It is the same as Form 13"Kick with Right Heel",only with left and right reversed.

第六组
Series Six

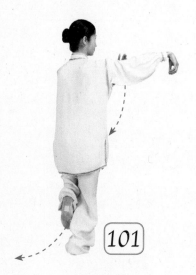

101

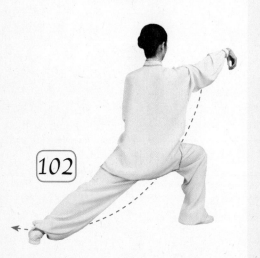

102

第十六式 左下势独立
Form 16 Push Down and Stand on One Leg (Left Style)

101 左腿屈收，左脚收于右小腿内侧；上体右转；右手变勾手，左手向右上划弧立于右肩前，手心斜向右；眼看勾手。

102 右腿屈膝半蹲，左脚前脚掌落地，然后沿地面向左侧伸出，随即左腿伸直，左脚全脚掌着地；同时左手立掌落于右肋前；眼看勾手。

❧ Withdraw the left leg,bending the knee,left foot is drawn to inner side of right lower leg;turn the torso to right;right hand turns into hooked hand,left hand is turned up to right in an arc to stand before right shoulder,heart of hand facing obliquely rightward.Eyes on hooked hand.(Fig.101)

❧ Half squat on right leg,the ball of left foot lands on the ground,and then stretch to left side along the ground and left leg stretches straight,left foot sets slightly firmly;while left hand to stand drops down to front of right ribs.Eyes on hooked hand. (Fig.102)

103 右腿屈膝全蹲，上体左转成左仆步；左手经腹前沿左腿内侧向前穿出，手心向右，指尖向前；眼看左手。

104 左脚尖外撇，屈膝前弓；右脚尖内扣，右腿自然蹬直，成左弓步；同时左手前穿至肩高，手心向右，右勾手内旋，背于身后，勾尖向上；眼看左手。

105 右腿提起成左独立步；同时左手下落按至左胯旁，手心向下；右勾手松开，右手经体侧向前挑起，手心向左，指尖与眼平，右肘与右膝上下相对；眼看右手。

☯ Crouch down on right leg,and then the torso turns to left to form a left crouching step;left hand past the front of abdomen extends forward along the inner side of left leg,with heart of hand facing rightward,fingertips pointing forward.Eyes on left hand.(Fig.103)

☯ Tiptoes of the left foot is turned outward and bend the left leg at knee to bow;the tiptoes of right foot is turned inward, meanwhile right leg straightens naturally to form a left bow step;at the same time,left hand extends forward to shoulder level,with heart of hand facing rightward,right hooked hand turns inward and stops behind the back of body,with bunched fingertips pointing upward.Eyes on left hand.(Fig.104)

☯ Raise right leg gradually,bending right knee to form a left independent step;at the same time,press the left hand downward beside the left hip,with heart of hand facing downward;turn the right hooked hand into palm,right hand past the side of body snaps up forward,heart of hand facing leftward,with the fingertips at the same level to eyes,right elbow is in vertical line with right knee.Eyes on right hand.(Fig.105)

要 点

右腿全蹲时，上体不可过于前倾。左腿伸直，左脚尖须向里扣，两脚掌全部着地，左脚尖与右脚跟踏在中轴线上。上体不可过于前倾。上体要正直，独立的腿要微屈，右腿提起时脚尖自然下垂。

Points to Remember

When full crouching down on right leg,the torso does not lean too much forward.When straightening left leg,tiptoes are turned inward,both soles flat fully on the ground and keep tiptoes of left in line with right heel;the torso does not lean too much forward.Keep the torso erect,the single standing leg should be slightly bent. When lifting right leg,tiptoes hang naturally downward.

第十七式　右下势独立

Form 17　Push Down and Stand on One Leg
(Right Style)

106 右脚掌着地，身体左转，左脚以脚掌为轴向左碾转；同时左手变勾手提于身体左侧，高与肩平；右手立掌落至左肩前，手心向左；眼看左手。

107 右脚收至左小腿内侧，然后右脚沿地面向右侧伸出，随即右腿伸直，右脚全脚掌着地；右手落至左胸侧；眼看勾手。

108 左腿屈膝全蹲，上体右转，成右仆步；同时右手经腹前沿右腿内侧向前穿出，手心向左，指尖向前；眼看右手。

❂ Place the sole of right foot down on the ground,turn body to left,left foot turns left,using left sole as a pivot;at the same time,left hand turns into hooked hand to raise to left side of body,at shoulder level;right hand to erect drops down to front of left shoulder,heart of hand facing leftward.Eyes on left hand.(Fig.106)

❂ Whithdraw right foot to the inner side of left lower leg,and then stretch right foot rightward along the ground, right leg stretches straight,right foot sets slightly firmly;while right hand drops to the side of left chest. Eyes on hooked hand. (Fig.107)

❂ Crouch down on left leg,the torso turns to right,to form a right crouching step;at the same time,right hand past the front of abdomen extends forward along the inner side of right leg, with heart of hand facing leftward,fingertips pointing forward. Eyes on right hand.(Fig.108)

109 右脚尖外撇，屈膝前弓；左脚尖内扣，左腿自然蹬直，成右弓步；同时右手前穿至肩高，手心向左，左勾手内旋，背于身后，勾尖向上；眼看右手。

110 左腿提起成右独立步；同时右手下落按至右胯旁，手心向下；左勾手松开，左手经体侧向前挑起，手心向右，指尖与眼平，左肘与左膝上下相对；眼看左手。

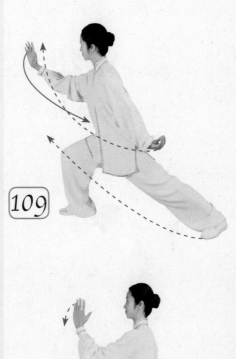

☯ Turn tiptoes of the right foot outward and bend the right leg at knee to bow forward;the tiptoes of left foot turned inward, meanwhile left leg straightens naturally to form a right bow step;at the same time,thread right hand forward to shoulder level,with heart of hand facing leftward,left hooked hand turns inward and stops behind the back of body,with bunched fingertips pointing upward.Eyes on right hand.(Fig.109)

☯ Raise left leg and stand on right leg to form a right independent step;at the same time,lower right hand to press at the side the right hip,with heart of hand facing downward;open left hooked hand and snap it forward past the side of body,with heart of hand facing rightward,fingertips at eyes level,left elbow is in vertical line with left knee.Eyes on left hand. (Fig.110)

要 点

右脚尖触地后必须稍微提起，然后再向下仆腿。其他均与"左下势独立"相同，惟左右相反。

Points to Remember

Tiptoes of right foot must be lifted a bit,after they touched the ground,then to crouch downward.other points are the same as Form 16 "Push Down and Stand on One Leg(Left Style)" only with left and right reversed.

第七组
Series Seven

111

112

第十八式　左右穿梭
Form 18　Work at Shuttles(Left-Right Style)

右穿梭
Work at Shuttles(Right Style)

111 左脚向左前方落步，脚跟着地，脚尖外撇，上体左转；左手内旋，手心翻转向下；眼看左手。

112 上体左转，左脚踏实，右脚收于左脚内侧点地，左腿半蹲；两手在左胸前成抱球状，左手心向下，右手翻转向上；眼看左手。

❷ Drop left foot forward to left,heel on the ground,tiptoes of left foot turned outward,the torso turns to left;left hand turns inward,heart of hand turned downward.Eyes on left hand. (Fig.111)

❷ The torso turns to left,Set left foot fimly,withdraw right foot beside left foot and tiptoes of right foot touch on the ground,left leg forms a half squat; while both hands form a hold-ball gesture in front of left chest, with heart of left hand facing downward,heart of right hand turned upward.Eyes on left hand.(Fig.112)

113
上体右转，右脚向右前方迈出，脚跟着地；同时右手由下向上方划弧，左手由上向后下方划弧；眼看右手。

114
上体继续右转，重心前移至右腿；右腿屈膝前弓，左腿自然蹬直成右弓步；右手向上翻转架于右额前，手心斜向上；左手向前推出，手心向前，手高与鼻平；眼看左手。

☻ The torso turns to right,right foot steps forward to right,heel on the ground;at the same time,right hand moves in an arc from lower place to upper place,left hand moves in an arc from top to lower rear.Eyes on right hand.(Fig.113)

☻ The torso goes on turning right,shift weight on right leg and bend the right leg at knee to bow forward,while straighten naturally left leg to form a right bow step;right hand turns upward,pausing just above right forehead,with heart of hand turned obliquely upward;push left hand forward,heart of hand facing forward,at nose level.Eyes on left hand.(Fig.114)

左穿梭
Work at Shuttles(Left Style)

115
重心稍后移，右脚尖稍外撇，身体右转；右手下落与肩平，左手稍向右划弧；眼看右手。

116
重心移至右腿，左脚收于右脚内侧，两手在右胸前成抱球状；眼看右手。

☻ Shift weight slightly backward,tiptoes of right foot turned slightly outward,turn body to right;right hand drops down to shoulder level,left hand moves in an arc to right slightly.Eyes on right hand.(Fig.115)

☻ Shift weight onto the right leg,left foot is withdrawn to inner side of the right foot,with tiptoes touching on the ground,both hands forming a right hold-ball gesure in front of right chest. Eyes on right hand.(Fig.116)

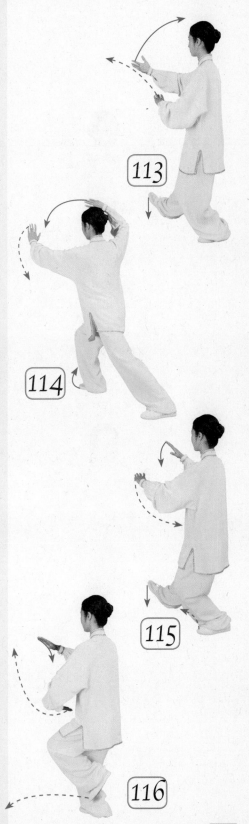

117 上体左转；左脚向左前方迈出，脚跟着地；同时左手由下向前上方划弧；右手由上向下方划弧；眼看左手。

118 上体继续左转，重心前移至左腿；左腿屈膝前弓，右腿自然蹬直成左弓步；左手向上翻转架于左额前，手心斜向上；右手向前推出，手心向前，手高与鼻平；眼看右手。

☯ The torso turns to left;left foot steps forward to left,the heel on the ground;at the same time,left hand moves in an arc from lower place to upper place;right hand moves in an arc from top to lower place.Eyes on left hand.(Fig.117)

☯ The torso goes on turning left,shift weight on left leg; left leg bend at knee to bow forward,while straighten naturally right leg to form a left bow step;left hand turns over upward to pause just above left forehead ,with heart of hand turned obliquely upward;push right hand forward,heart of hand facing forward,at nose level.Eyes on right hand.(Fig.118)

要 点

手推出后，上体不可前俯。手向上举时，防止引肩上耸。一手上举一手前推要与弓腿松腰协调一致。做弓步时，两脚跟的横向距离保持在30厘米左右。

Points to Remember

When pushing hands out,torso does not lean forward.Do not shrug your shoulder while raising hand,and when pushing forward,the speed upraising hand and pushing hand should be coordinated with legs bent and waist relaxed.In forming bow step,the transverse distance between heels is about 30cm.

第十九式　海底针

Form 19　Needle at Sea Bottom

119 上体稍右转，右脚向前半步，脚前掌落地；眼看前方。

120 重心由左腿移至右腿，左脚跟提起；右手下落经体前向上提抽至耳旁，手心向左，指尖向前；左手向右划弧下落至腹前，手心向下，指尖斜向右；眼看前方。

121 上体稍左转，右腿屈膝，左脚尖点地成左虚步；右手向前下方下插，手心向左，指尖斜向下；左手经左膝前划弧搂过，按至大腿外侧，左脚稍前移，脚前掌着地成左虚步；眼看右手。

119

120

121

❧ The torso turns slightly to right,take right foot half a step forward,the ball of the foot on the ground.Eyes front. (Fig.119)

❧ Shift weight from left leg to right leg,left heel lifted off the ground;right hand drops past front of body and then to raise and withdraw it upward to side of right ear,heart of hand facing leftward,fingertips pointing forward;left hand makes an arc to right,droping to front of abdomen,heart of hand facing downward,fingertips pointing obliquely rightward.Eyes front.(Fig.120)

❧ The torso turns to left slightly,right leg bend at knee, tiptoes of left foot touch on the ground to form a left empty step;thrust right hand to lower-front,heart of hand facing leftward,with fingertips pointing obliquely downward;left hand brushes over left knee in an arc,to press to the outer side of the leg,left foot moves slightly forward,the ball of the foot touching the ground to form a left empty step.Eyes on right hand.(Fig.121)

要　点

身体要先向右转，再向左转。上体不可太前倾。避免低头和臀部外凸。左腿要微屈。

Points to Remember

Turn body first right,and then left.Torso does not lean too much forward,avoid to bend head and jut buttocks out.Left leg should be slightly bent.

第二十式　闪通臂
Form 20　Flash the Arms

122 上体稍右转，起身至正直，坐实右腿，左脚回收，以脚尖点地落至右脚内侧；右手上提至肩平，手心向左，指尖向前；左臂屈收，指尖贴近右腕内侧；眼看前方。

123 左脚向前迈出，脚跟着地，两手翻转成手心向前；眼看前方。

124 上体右转，重心前移成左弓步，右手上提撑于头侧上方，掌心翻转斜向外；左手向前推出，手心向前，高与鼻尖平；眼看左手。

❷ Uprise the torso upright and turn body slightly to right,sit firmly on right leg,withdraw left leg inward,beside right foot with tiptoes touching on the ground;right hand is lifted upward to the shoulder level,heart of hand facing leftward,with fingertips pointing forward;left arm is bent,the fingers of it resting on inside of right wrist.Eyes front. (Fig.122)

❷ Left foot steps forward,the heel lands on the ground,while both hands turned to hearts of hands facing forward.Eyes front. (Fig.123)

❷ The torso turns to right,shift weight forward to form left bow step,raise right hand to pause just above the right temple, with heart of hand facing obliquely outward;meanwhile push left hand forward,heart of hand facing forward,at tip of nose level. Eyes on left hand.(Fig.124)

要　点

上体自然正直、松腰、松胯，左臂不要完全伸直，背部肌肉要伸展开。推掌、举掌和弓腿动作要协调一致。

Points to Remember

Hold torso erect in a natural position with waist and hips relaxed.Do not straighten left arm.Keep spinal muscles extended. Movements pushing palms,raising palms and bending legs should be coordinated.

第二十一式　转身搬拦捶

Form 21　Turn Over,Deflect Downward,Parry and Punch

125 重心移至右腿，左脚尖内扣，身体右转；两臂向右侧摆动，右手摆至身体右侧，左手摆至头侧，两手心均向外；眼看右手。

126 重心左移，左腿屈坐，右脚以脚掌为轴扭直；右手握拳向下、向左划弧收于左肋前，拳心向下；左手撑举于左额前上方，手心斜向上；眼看前方。

127 右脚提收至左脚内侧，再向前迈出，脚跟着地，脚尖外撇；右拳经体前向右前搬压，拳心向上，高与肩平，肘部微屈；左手经右前臂外侧下落，按至左胯旁，手心向下，指尖向前；眼看右拳。

◐ Shift weight onto right leg,with tiptoes of left foot turned inward,the body turns to right;both arms swing to side right,right hand swings to right side of the body,left hand swings to side of head,hearts of hands completely outward.Eyes on right hand.(Fig.125)

◐ Shift weight to left,sit left leg bent at knee,right foot turns straight as pivot of the ball of right foot;clench right hand into a fist to move in a downward-leftwatd arc and withdraw it to front of left ribs,heart of fist facing downward;left hand raises up to left forehead to upper front,heart of hand facing obliquely upward.Eyes front.(Figs.126A, 126B)

◐ Withdraw right foot to the inner side of left foot and then step forward,the heel on the ground,tiptoes of right foot turned outward;right fist deflects and presses past the front of body forward to right,heart of fist facing upward,at shoulder level,elbow is bent slightly;left hand drops down past the outer side of right forearm,and press beside left hip,heart of hand facing downward,fingertips pointing forward.Eyes on right fist.(Fig.127)

第八组

Series Eight

125

126B

126A

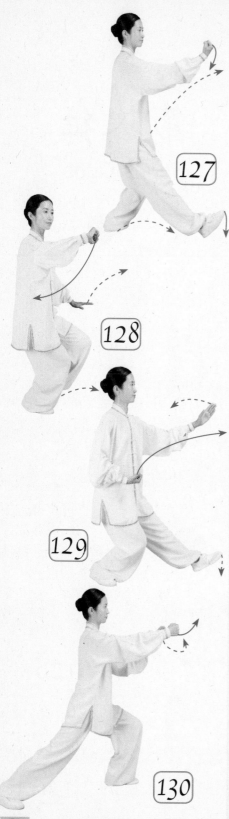

128 上体右转，重心前移至右腿，左脚收于右脚内侧；右拳向右划弧至体侧，拳心向下；左臂外旋，左手经左侧向体前划弧；眼平视右拳。

129 左脚向前上步，脚跟着地，左手拦至体前与肩平，手心向右，指尖斜向上；右拳翻转收至右腰旁，拳心向上；眼看左手。

130 上体左转，重心前移，左腿屈弓，左脚踏实，右腿自然蹬直，成左弓步；同时右拳自胸前打出，拳心转向左，拳眼向上，左手附于右前臂内侧，手心向右；眼看右拳。

❂ The torso turns to right,shift weight forward onto right leg,withdraw left foot beside right foot;right fist moves in a rightward arc to the front of body,heart of fist facing downward; left arm turns outward,left hand moves in an arc past left side to front of body.Eyes looking at right fist.(Fig.128)

❂ Left foot takes a step forward,the heel on the ground, meanwhile,parry with left hand to front of the body,at shoulder level,heart of hand facing rightward,fingertips pointing obliquely upward;right fist is turned over to withdraw beside right waist,heart of fist facing upward. Eyes on left hand. (Fig.129)

❂ The torso turns to left,shift weight forward,left leg is bent at knee to bow,sets left foot firmly,while straighten naturally right leg to form a left bow step;at the same time,punch the right fist forward from the front of chest,heart of the fist turns leftward,eye of the fist facing upward;left hand beside the inner side of right forearm,heart of hand facing rightward.Eyes on right fist.(Fig.130)

要 点

右拳不要握得太紧。右拳回收时，前臂先慢慢内旋后收，再外旋停于右腰旁，拳心向上。向前打拳时，右肩随拳略向前引伸，沉肩垂肘，右臂微屈。

Points to Remember

Clench right fist loosely.Right forearm turns inward first gradually and withdraws it backward,then turns it outward again, ending beside right side of waist,heart of fist upward.While the fist strikes forward,right shoulder should follow the movement and extend a bit forward.Keep shoulder and elbow low with right arm slightly bent.

第二十二式　如封似闭

Form 22　Apparent Close-up

131 左手翻转向上，从右前臂下向前穿出；同时右拳松开，两手心均向上交叉于体前，与肩同高；眼看前方。

132 重心后移，右腿屈坐，左脚尖翘起；两臂屈收内旋至胸前，与肩同宽，手心斜向下；眼看前方。

133 重心前移，左腿屈弓，左脚踏实，右腿自然蹬直成左弓步；两手经腹前向上、向前推出，与肩同宽，腕高与肩平，手心向前；眼看前方。

❧ Turn left hand upward,and then it extends forward from below right forearm;which opens into a palm,both palms turn upward completely and cross to front of body,at shoulder level. Eyes front.(Fig.131)

❧ Shift weight backward,right leg is bent to sit,with toes of left foot raised;both arms withdraw back and turn inward to front of chest,keeping shoulder-width apart,hearts of hands facing obliquely downward.Eyes front.(Fig.132)

❧ Shift weight forward,left leg is bent at knee to bow,left foot sets firmly,right leg straightens naturally to form a left bow step;both hands push out past the front of abdomen upward and forward,keeping shoulder-width apart,wrists at shoulder level,hearts of hands facing forward.Eyes front.(Fig.133)

要　点

　　身体后坐时，避免后仰，臀部不可凸出。两臂随身体回收时，肩、肘部略向外松开，不要直着抽回，两手推出宽度不要超过两肩。

Points to Remember

When body sits back,avoid torso to lean backward,Buttocks would not jut out.While withdrawing both arms,let shoulders and elbows extend freely outward a little, and not withdrawing straight back.The extended hands should be no farther than shoulder-width apart.

131

132

133

第二十三式 十字手
Form 23　Cross Hands

134 上体右转，重心右移至右腿，左脚尖内扣；右手向右划弧摆至头前；眼看右手。

135 上体继续右转，右脚尖外撇，右腿屈弓，左腿自然蹬直，成右侧弓步；右手向右划弧，摆至身体右侧，两手分至两侧与肩同高，手心皆向外，指尖斜向上；眼看右手。

☯ The torso turns to right,shift weight onto right leg,tiptoes of left foot turned inward;right hand swings rightward to the front of the head in an arc.Eyes on right hand.(Fig.134)

☯ The torso goes on turning to right,tiptoes of right foot turned outward,right leg is bent at knee,left leg straightens naturally to form a side bow step;right hand moves in rightward arc,to swing to right side of body,both hands are separated on both sides at shoulder level,hearts of hands completely outward, fingertips pointing obliquely upward.Eyes on right hand. (Fig.135)

136 上体左转，重心左移，屈弓左腿，右腿自然伸直，脚尖内扣；两手下落划弧，抱于胸前，右手在外，两手心向内；眼平视前方。

137 重心移至左腿，右脚尖内扣；再向左收回，与肩同宽，随之全脚踏实，两脚平行向前，体重平均于两腿之间；两手下落划弧，在腹前交叉上抱于胸前；两臂撑圆，掌心向内，腕与肩高；两腿慢慢直立；眼平视前方。

☯ The torso turns to left,shift weight to left,left leg is bent to bow,right leg straightens naturally,tiptoes of right foot turned inward;both hands are lowered and crossed in an arc before chest,the right in front of the left,hearts of hands facing inward.Eyes looking straight forward.(Fig.136)

☯ Shift weight onto left leg,tiptoes of right foot turned inward;and then withdraw right foot towards left foot,keep feet with shoulder-width apart,both feet flat on the ground firmly in a parallel stance forward,weight of body is equally distributed between two legs;both hands drop down in an arc and cross them before abdomen then up to front of chest,both arms are rounded,hearts of hands facing inward,with wrists at shoulder level;both legs stand gradually upright.Eyes looking straight forward.(Fig.137)

136

137

要 点

两手分开和合抱时，上体不要前俯。站起后，身体自然正直，头要微上顶，下颏稍向后收。两臂环抱时须圆满舒适，沉肩垂肘。

Points to Remember

Do not lean forward when separating or crossing hands.After stand up,keep body naturally erect,with head straight and chin slightly in.Keep both arms rounded in a comfortable position, with shoulders and elbows down.

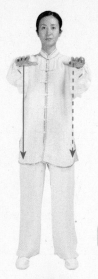

138

第二十四式　收势
Form 24 Closing Form

138 两臂内旋，两手翻转左右分开，手心向下，与肩同宽；眼平视前方。

139 两臂徐徐下垂，两手落于大腿外侧；眼平视前方。

140 左脚轻轻提起与右脚并拢，脚前掌先着地，随之全脚踏实，恢复成预备姿势；眼看前方。

139

❷ Turn both arms inward,turn both hands to the side of the left and the right,hearts of hands facing downward,shoulder-width apart. Eyes looking straight forward.(Fig.138)

❷ Gradually drop both arms downward in arcs until the hands are to the outer sides of both legs. Eyes looking straight forward.(Fig.139)

❷ Lift gently left foot close to right foot,the ball of the foot touching the ground first,and then foot flat firmly, return to preparatory posture.Eyes front.(Fig.140)

要　点

两手左右分开下落时，全身注意放松，同时气徐徐向下沉（呼气略加长）。呼吸平稳后，把左腿收到右脚旁，再走动休息。

Points to Remember

While separating and lowering both hands to the side of the left and the right,keep whole body relaxed and sink breath into abdomen(exhalation prolonged a bit). Withdraw left foot close to right foot after your breath is even.Then have a walk for rest.

140

式太极拳竞赛套路

Competition Routine of 42 Forms Taiji Quan

绵绵不断
轻松柔和
圆活自然

第一式　起势

Form 1　Starting Posture

1 身体自然直立，两脚并拢，头颈端正，下颏稍内收，胸腹舒松，肩臂松垂，两手轻贴大腿两侧；精神集中，呼吸自然，目平视前方。

2 左脚向左轻轻开步，相距与肩同宽，脚尖向前。

3 两手慢慢向前平举，与肩同高，掌心向下，两肘稍下垂，两臂相距与肩同宽。

4 上体保持正直，两腿缓缓屈膝半蹲，两掌轻轻下按，落于腹前，掌与膝相对。

❂ Stand upright naturally with feet together.Hold head and neck erect with chin withdrawn slightly inward.Keep chest and abdomen relaxed.Hold shoulders and elbows down with arms hanging naturally,hands touching the sides of thighs gently. Concentrate your thoughts on every movement you perform and breath naturally.Eyes looking straight forward.(Fig.1)

❂ Take a step gently to left so that feet are shoulder-width apart,tiptoes pointing forward.(Fig.2)

❂ Raise hands slowly forward to shoulder level,hearts of palms facing downward and elbows dropped slightly. Keep arms shoulder-width apart.(Fig.3)

❂ Keep the torso upright and bend knees slowly to half squat,while pressing palms gently down to front of abdomen, palms are in vertical line with knees.(Fig.4)

第二式　右揽雀尾

Form 2　Grasp the Bird's Tail(Right Style)

5 右脚尖稍外撇，同时身体微向右转，右臂上抬屈于胸前，掌心向下；左掌翻转向右划弧至右腹前，与右掌相对如抱球状；重心移至右腿，左脚收于右脚内侧；目视右掌。

6 上体微左转，左脚向左前方上一步，脚跟轻轻落地。

7 上体继续左转，重心前移屈弓左膝，自然蹬直右腿成左弓步；同时左臂向前掤出，左掌高与肩平，掌心向内；右掌向下落于右胯旁，掌心向下，指尖向前，两臂微屈；目视左前臂。

❂ Tiptoes of right foot slightly turn outward,while body turns right a little,right arm is bent an even arc up to the front of chest,heart of right palm facing downward;left palm turns rightward in an arc to front of right abdomen,to face right palm each other forming a hold-ball gesture;weight is shifted on to right leg and left foot is withdrawn beside the inner side of right foot.Eyes on right palm.(Fig.5)

❂ The torso turns slightly to left,left foot takes a step forward to left,with the heel landing on the ground gently. (Fig.6)

❂ The torso goes on turning to left,shift weight forward to bend left knee,meanwhile straighten right leg naturally to form a left bow step;at the same time,left arm thrusts forward with palm at shoulder level,heart of palm facing inward;right palm drops downward beside right hip,heart of palm facing downward, fingertips pointing forward,both arms slightly bent.Eyes on left forearm.(Fig.7)

8 上体微左转，右脚收至左脚内侧；左臂内旋屈于左胸前，左掌与肩同高，掌心向下，指尖向右；右臂向左划弧至左腹前，掌心向上，指尖向左，两手相对如抱球状，目视左掌。

9 上体微右转，右脚向右前方轻轻迈出一步，脚跟着地。

10 上体继续右转，重心前移屈弓右膝，自然蹬直左腿成右弓步；同时右臂向前掤出，右掌高与肩平，掌心向内；左掌向下落于左胯旁，掌心向下，两臂稍屈；目视右前臂。

11 上体微右转，右掌前伸，掌心翻转向下；左掌同时翻转向上，伸至右腕下方，目视右掌。

❀ The torso turns to left a little,withdraw right foot beside left foot;meanwhile left arm turns inward and bends an even arc before left chest,left palm is at shoulder level,heart of palm facing downward,fingertips pointing rightward;right arm moves in a leftward arc to front of left abdomen,heart of palm facing upward,fingertips pointing leftward,both hands face each other as if forming a hold-ball gesture.Eyes on left palm.(Fig.8)

❀ The torso turns slightly to right,right foot takes a step forward to right,with the heel landing on the ground gently. (Fig.9)

❀ The torso goes on turning to right,shift weight forward to bend at right knee,meanwhile straighten left leg naturally to form a rihgt bow step;at the same time,right arm thrusts forward,with palm at shoulder level,heart of palm facing inward;left palm drops downward beside left hip,heart of palm facing downward,and both arms slightly bent.Eyes on right forearm.(Fig.10)

❀ The torso turns to right slightly,right palm extends forward, turning heart of palm downward;while left palm turns up and extends under right wrist.Eyes on right palm. (Fig.11)

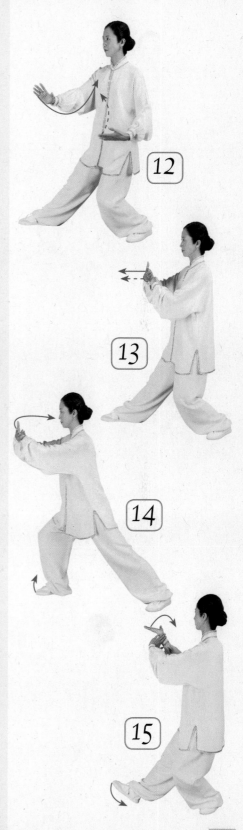

12 重心后移，上体微左转；双掌向下后捋至腹前；目随右掌。

13 右臂外旋屈肘于胸前，右掌心向内，指尖向左；左臂内旋，左掌心转向外，左掌指附于右腕内侧。

14 重心前移，成右弓步，两掌同时向前挤出，两臂撑圆；目视前方。

15 重心后移，上体微右转；右脚尖上翘；右臂外旋，右掌心翻转向上，自前向右、向后屈肘划平弧至右肩前；左掌仍附于右腕内侧随之划弧；目随右掌。

❂ Shift weight backward and the torso turns to left a little;while stroke both palms downward to front of abdomen. Eyes following right palm.(Fig.12)

❂ Right arm turns outward to bend elbow an even arc to front of chest,heart of right palm facing inward,fingertips pointing leftward;left arm turns inward,with heart of palm facing outward,fingers rest on the inner side of right wrist.(Fig.13)

❂ Shift weight forward to form a right bow step;at the same time,push both palms forward,arms rounded.Eyes front.(Fig.14)

❂ The weight is shifted backward,the torso turns to right a little,tiptoes of right foot raised;right arm turns outward, heart of right palm turned upward,from front of right and rear, bending elbow in an even arc to front of right shoulder;left palm rests still on the inner side of right wrist to follow in arc.Eyes following right palm.(Fig.15)

16 身体左转，右脚尖内扣；右掌平旋内收。

17 上体微右转，重心右移，左脚收至右脚内侧，脚尖着地成"丁"步；右臂内旋，右掌翻转向右前方立掌按出，腕与肩平，掌心向外；左掌随之翻转向内，指尖仍附于右腕侧；目视右掌。

❶ The body turns to left,tiptoes of right foot turned inward,right palm is withdrawn inward in an even curve.(Fig.16)

❶ The torso turns right a little,shift weight to right, withdraw left foot inside right foot,tiptoes on the ground forming T-step;right arm is turned inward,right palm is turned forward to right and stand it to push out,the wrist at shoulder level,heart of palm facing outward;while left palm turned inward,the fingertips rest still on the side of right wrist.Eyes on right palm.(Fig.17)

第三式　左单鞭
Form 3　Left Single Whip

18 上体微左转，左脚向左前方上一步，脚跟着地；右掌变勾手；左掌向左划弧至面前；目视左掌。

19 上体继续左转；重心前移，成左弓步；左前臂内旋，左掌翻转向前推出，掌心向前，腕高与肩平；目视左掌。

❶ The torso turns to left a little,left foot takes a step forward to left,the heel landing on the ground ;right palm turns into a hooked hand;left palm moves in a leftward curve to front of face.Eyes on left palm.(Fig.18)

❶ The torso goes on turning to left;shift weight forward to form a left bow step;left forearm turns inward and pushes out,with left palm turning over,heart of palm facing forward,with wrist at shoulder level.Eyes on left palm.(Fig.19)

第四式　提手

Form 4　Raise Hands

20 重心后坐，上体右转，左脚尖内扣，左掌向右平摆划弧；目视左掌。

21 重心左移，右勾手变掌，左掌稍向左平带。

22 上体微右转，右脚提转，脚跟落地，脚尖上翘，成右虚步；右掌成侧立掌举于体前，指尖高与眉齐；左臂屈收，左手也成侧立掌合于右肘内侧；目视右掌。

❶ Sit weight back and turn the torso to right,tiptoes of left foot turned inward,while left palm swings to right in an even arc.Eyes on left palm.(Fig.20)

❶ Shift weight to left,right hooked hand turns into palm,left palm withdraws leftward back a little in even curve.(Fig.21)

❶ The torso turns to right a little,right foot is lifted to shift,heel on the ground,with tiptoes off ground to form a right empty step;right palm turns into side-standing palm to raise before the body with fingertips at eyebrow level;left arm is bent and withdrawn,with left hand also turning into side-standing palm to close to the inner side of right elbow. Eyes on right palm.(Fig.22)

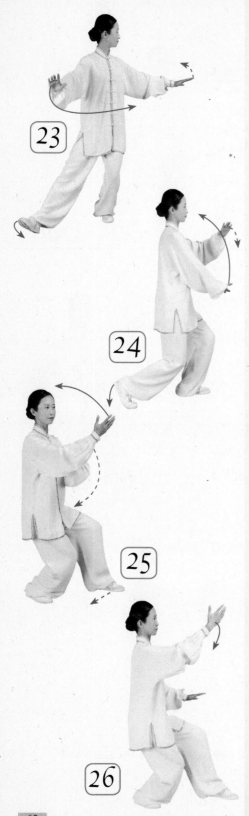

第五式　白鹤亮翅
Form 5　White Crane Spreads Its Wings

23 上体左转，两手向左方划弧分开；目视前方。

24 右脚活步移动，脚尖内扣落地；右手继续向左下方划弧翻转，两手抱于左胸前，左手在上，两臂微屈成弧形；目视左手。

25 重心右移，上体右转，两手边合边举至右肩前；目视右掌。

26 上体微左转，左脚稍向内收，脚尖点地成左虚步；两手右上左下划弧分开，右掌提至右额前，掌心向左；左掌按于左胯旁，掌心向下，两臂保持弧形；目平视前方。

◎ The torso turns to left,both hands are spreaded to left in an arc.Eyes front.(Fig.23)

◎ Right foot takes free moving step to shift,tiptoes of right foot inward to land on the ground,right hand continue to turn to lower-left in an arc and then both hands turn to close to front of left chest,left hand on top,both arms are bent slightly to form an arc.Eyes on left hand.(Fig.24)

◎ Shift weight to right,the torso turns to right,meanwhile hands close and raise to front of right shoulder.Eyes on right palm.(Fig.25)

◎ The torso turns slightly to left,left foot is withdrawn inward a little,tiptoes of left foot on the ground to form a left empty step;both hands separate in an up to right and down to left curve,the right palm comes up to front of right forehead, heart of palm facing leftward;left palm presses beside the left hip,heart of palm facing downward,keep both arms in an arc.Eyes looking straight forward.(Fig.26)

第六式　搂膝拗步

Form 6　Brush Knee and Twist Step
(Left-Right Style)

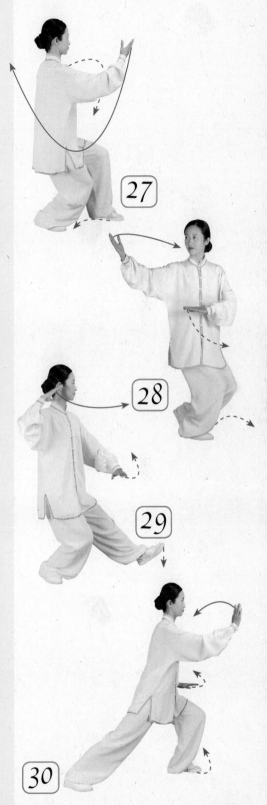

27 上体微左转；右手随之向左划弧自头前下落；目视右手。

28 上体右转，随之右手向下、向右、向上划弧至右前方，高与头平，手心斜向上；左手向上、向右、向下划弧至右肋旁，手心向下；左脚收至右脚内侧；目视右手。

29 上体左转，左脚向前上步，脚跟轻轻落地；右臂屈肘，右手收至耳旁，掌心斜向前；左手向下划弧至腹前；目视前方。

30 重心前移，成左弓步；右手成立掌向前推出，指尖高与鼻平；左手由左膝前搂过，按于左胯旁；目视右掌。

❀ The torso turns slightly to left as right hand moves to left in a curve to drop down from the front of head.Eyes on right hand.(Fig.27)

❀ The torso turns to right while right hand moves in a downward-rightward-upward arc to front-right,at head level, heart of hand facing obliquely upward;left hand moves in an upward-rightward-downward arc to side of right ribs,heart of hand facing downward;left foot is withdrawn to the inner side of right foot.Eyes on right hand.(Fig.28)

❀ The torso turns to left,left foot takes a step forward,the heel on the ground gently;bend right arm at elbow,right hand is withdrawn to the side of right ear,heart of palm facing obliquely forward;left hand moves downward in an arc to front of abdomen.Eyes front.(Fig.29)

❀ Shift weight forward to form a left bow step;meanwhlie right hand turns into a standing palm and then pushes out forward,fingertips at nose level;left hand brushes over left knee,presses beside left hip.Eyes on right palm.(Fig.30)

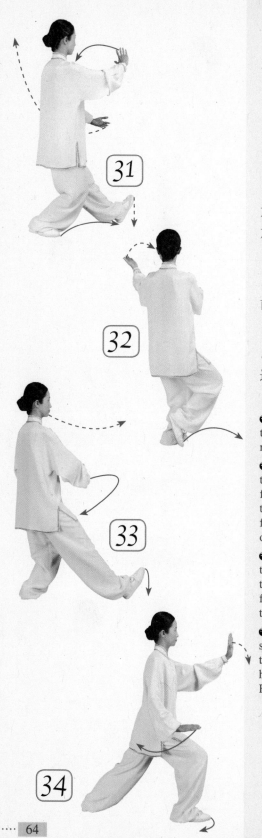

31 重心稍后移，左脚尖外撇，上体左转；右手随之向左划弧；目随右手。

32 左手向左、向上划弧，举至身体左前方，高与头平，手心斜向上；右手摆至左肋旁，手心向下；右脚收至左脚内侧；目视左手。

33 上体右转，右脚向前上步，脚跟轻轻落地；左臂屈肘，左手收至耳旁，手心斜向前；右手向右、向下划弧至腹前；目视前方。

34 重心前移，成右弓步；左手成立掌向前推出，指尖高与鼻平，右手由右膝前搂过，按于右胯旁；目视左掌。

☯ Shift weight backward slightly,tiptoes of left foot turned outward;the torso turns to left;while right hand moves to left in an arc.Eyes follow right hand.(Fig.31)

☯ Left hand moves in a leftward-upward arc,to raise up to left front of the body,at head level,with heart of hand facing obliquely upward; meanwhile right hand swings to the side of left ribs,heart of hand facing downward;right foot is withdrawn to the inner side of the left foot.Eyes on left hand.(Fig.32)

☯ The torso turns to right,right foot takes a step forward, the heel on the ground gently;left arm is withdrawn to the side of left ear,heart of hand facing obliquely forward;right hand moves in a rightward-downward arc to front of abdomen.Eyes front.(Fig.33)

☯ Shift weight forward to form a right bow step;meanwhile left hand turns into a standing palm and then pushes out forward,fingertips at nose level;right hand brushes over right knee,presses beside right hip. Eyes on left palm.(Fig.34)

第七式　撇身捶

Form 7　Sidle to Punch

35 重心稍后移，右脚尖外撇，上体右转；左手向左前伸展，手心向下，右前臂外旋，右手向右后方划弧分开；目视左手。

36 右脚踏实，左脚收于右脚内侧；左手握拳，下落于小腹前，拳心向内，拳眼向右，右手向上、向体前划弧，附于左前臂内侧，手心向下；目视左前方。

37 上体微左转，左脚向左前方上一步，脚跟着地；左拳上举至面前。

38 重心前移，成左弓步；左拳翻转向前撇打，拳心斜向上，高与头平，右手仍附于左前臂内侧；目视左拳。

❀ Shift weight backward slightly,tiptoes of right foot turned outward,the torso turns to right;left hand extends forward to left,heart of hand facing downward;at the same time,right forearm turns outward with right hand separating to rear-right in an arc.Eyes on left hand.(Fig.35)

❀ Set right foot firmly,left foot is withdrawn to the inner side of the right foot; clench left hand into fist and drop it to front of abdomen,with heart of fist facing inward and eye of fist facing rightward, right hand moves in an upward, and to front of body arc to rest on the inner side of left forearm,heart of hand facing downward. Eyes on front-left.(Fig.36)

❀ The torso turns to left slightly,left foot takes a step forward to left,with heel on the ground;meanwhile left fist goes up to front of face.(Fig.37)

❀ Shift weight forward to form a left bow step;left fist is turned forward to sidle and punch,heart of fist obliquely upward,at head level;right hand still rests on the inner side of left forearm.Eyes on left fist.(Fig.38)

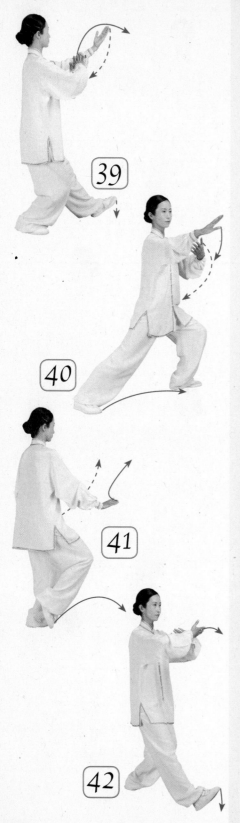

第八式　捋挤势

Form 8　Stroke and Push

39 重心稍后移，左脚尖内扣，上体右转；左拳变掌，右掌向右划一平弧，随即收于左前臂内侧。

40 重心前移，上体继续右转；右掌由左向右前方划弧平抹，掌心斜向下；左掌落于右肘内侧下方，掌心斜向上；目视右掌。

41 两掌自前同时向下、向后捋，左掌捋至左胯旁，右掌捋至腹前；右脚收至左脚内侧；目视右前方。

42 右脚向右前方上步，脚跟着地；同时左前臂内旋，右前臂外旋，两手翻转屈臂上举，收于胸前，手心相对；目视前方。

◉ Shift weight slightly backward,tiptoes of left foot turned inward,the torso turns to right;meanwhile left fist turns into palm,right palm moves to right in an even arc and then withdrawn to the inner side of left forearm.(Fig.39)

◉ Shift weight forward,the torso continues to turn to right; right palm moves from left to front-right in a rounded horizontal arc,heart of palm facing obliquely downward;left palm drops under the inner side of right elbow,heart of palm facing obliquely upward.Eyes on right palm.(Fig.40)

◉ Stroke both palms from the front while in a downward-backward curve,left palm strokes beside left hip, right palm stroks to the front of abdomen;right foot is withdrawn to the inner side of left foot.Eyes on right-front. (Fig.41)

◉ Right foot takes a step forward to right,heel on the ground; while left forearm turns inward and right forearm turns outward,both hands turn and both arms bent to raise up,to close before chest,heart of hands facing each other. Eyes front. (Fig.42)

43 重心前移，成右弓步；两臂同时向前挤出，两臂撑圆，左掌指贴于右腕内侧，掌心向外，指尖斜向上；右掌心向内，指尖向左，高与肩平；目视右掌。

44 重心后移，右脚尖内扣，上体左转；右掌翻转向上，左掌划一小弧从右前臂穿出。

45 重心前移，上体继续左转；左掌自右向左前方划弧平抹，掌心斜向下；右掌收于左肘内侧下方，掌心斜向上；目视左掌。

46 两掌自前同时向下、向后捋，右掌捋至右胯旁，左掌捋至腹前；左脚收至右脚内侧；目视左前方。

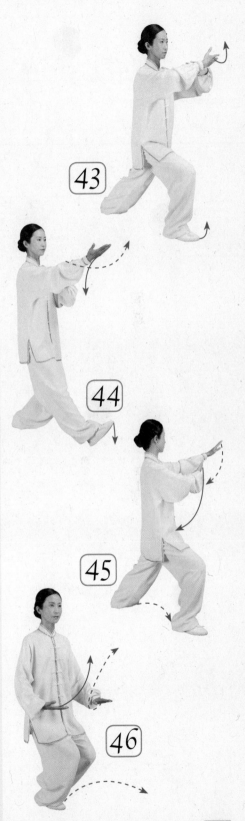

◑ Shift weight forward to form a right bow step;at the same time,push out both arms forward,arms rounded,left fingers close to the inner of right wrist,heart of palm facing outward with fingertips pointing obliquely upward;heart of right palm facing inward with fingertips pointing leftward,at shoulder level.Eyes on right palm.(Fig.43)

◑ Shift weight backward,tiptoes of right foot turned inward, the torso turns to left;right palm turns upward,left palm threads over right forearm in a small arc.(Fig.44)

◑ Shift weight forward and the torso continues to turn left;left palm moves from right to front-left in a rounded horizontal curve,heart of palm facing obliquely downward;right palm is withdrawn below the inner side of left elbow,heart of palm facing obliquely upward.Eyes on left palm.(Fig.45)

◑ Stroke both palms from the front while in a downward-backward curve,right palm strokes beside right hip, left palm stroks to the front of abdomen;left foot is withdrawn to the inner side of right foot.Eyes on left-front.(Fig.46)

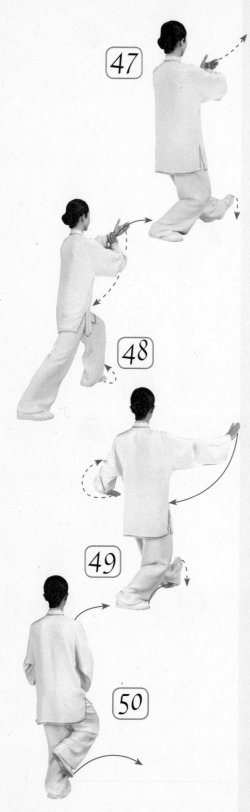

47 左脚向左前方上一步，脚跟着地；同时右前臂内旋，左前臂外旋，两手翻转屈臂上举收于胸前，手心相对；目视前方。

48 重心前移，成左弓步；右掌指贴于左腕内侧，两臂向前挤出，高与肩平；目视左掌。

❀ Left foot takes a step forward to left,heel on the ground; while right forearm turns inward,left forearm outward,both hands turn over and arms bent to raise up to close to front of chest,hearts of hands facing each other. Eyes front.(Fig.47)

❀ Shift weight forward to form a left bow step;right fingers rest on the inner side of left wrist,push out both arms forward,at shoulder level.Eyes on left palm.(Fig.48)

第九式　进步搬拦捶
Form 9　Step Up,Deflect Downward,Parry and Punch

49 重心后移，左脚尖外撇，上体左转；左掌向下划弧，掌心向上；右掌向右前方伸展，掌心斜向下；头随上体转动。

50 重心前移，右脚收于左脚内侧；左掌向左划弧，再向上卷收于体前，掌心向下；右掌变拳向下划弧收于腹前，拳心向下；目向前平视。

❀ Shift weight backward,tiptoes of left foot turned outward, the torso turns to left;meanwhile left palm moves downward in a curve,heart of palm facing upward;right palm extends forward to right,heart of palm facing obliquely downward.Head follows the movement of body.(Fig.49)

❀ Shift weight forward,withdraw right foot beside left foot;left palm moves leftward in an arc and then pull it back and upward to the front of body,heart of palm facing downward;clench right palm into a fist to move in downward arc to draw it to the front of abdomen,heart of fist facing downward. Eyes looking straight forward.(Fig.50)

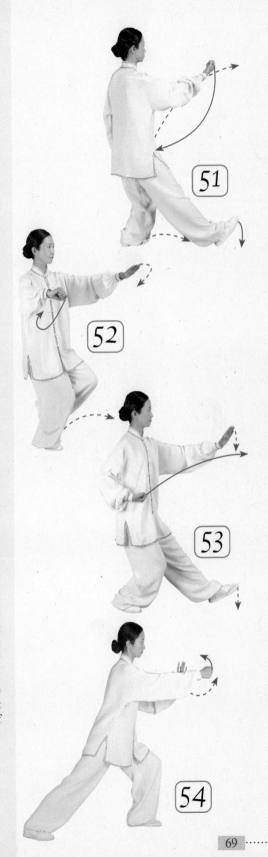

51 右脚向前上步，脚跟着地，脚尖外撇；右拳随之经左臂内侧向前翻转搬出，拳心向上，高与胸平；左掌顺势按至左胯旁；目视右拳。

52 重心前移，上体右转，左脚收于右脚内侧；右前臂内旋，右拳向右划弧至体侧，左前臂外旋，左掌向左向前划弧至体前；目视左掌。

53 左脚向前一步，脚跟落地；右拳收于右腰间，拳心向上，左掌翻转向下，拦于体前；目视左掌。

54 重心前移，成左弓步；右拳向前打出，拳眼转向上，高与胸齐，左掌收于右前臂内侧；目视右拳。

❀ Right foot takes a step forward with heel on the ground, tiptoes of right foot turned outward;right fist turns and thrusts out forward past the inner of left arm,heart of fist facing upward,at chest level;while left palm presses beside left hip.Eyes on right fist.(Fig.51)

❀ Shift weight forward,the torso turns to right,withdraw left foot beside right foot;while right forearm turns inward, right fist moves in rightward curve to the side of body,left forearm turns outward,left palm moves in a curve forward to left to front of body.Eyes on left palm.(Fig.52)

❀ Left foot takes a step forward,heel on the ground;right fist is withdrawn to the part of right waist,heart of fist facing upward ,left palm turns downward to parry an imaginary blow before the body.Eyes on left palm.(Fig.53)

❀ Shift weight forward to form a left bow step;while right fist strikes forward,heart of fist turning upward,at chest level,left palm is withdrawn to the inner side of right forearm. Eyes on right fist.(Fig.54)

第十式　如封似闭
Form 10　Apparent Close-up

55 左掌从右前臂下穿出，掌心向上；右拳随之变掌，掌心也转向上。

56 上体后坐，重心后移，左脚尖上翘；两掌分开并屈臂内旋，收至胸前，与肩同宽，掌心斜相对。

57 两掌翻转向下，落至腹前；目视前方。

58 重心前移，右脚收至左脚内侧后方，脚尖点地，与左脚相距约10厘米，成右"丁"步；两掌向前按出，与肩同宽，掌心向前，腕与肩平；目视两掌。

❧ Left palm extends out from below right forearm,heart of palm facing upward;while open right fist into a palm,heart of palm facing upward too.(Fig.55)

❧ The torso sits back and shift weight backward,tiptoes of left foot raised;separate both palms and both arms are bent to turn inward, withdraw to the front of chest,being shoulder-width apart,hearts of palms facing obliquely each other.(Fig.56)

❧ Both palms turn downward and drop to the front of abdomen. Eyes front.(Fig.57)

❧ Shift weight forward,withdraw right foot behind the inner side of left foot,with tiptoes touching on the ground,and it is apart about 10cm of left foot,forming a right T-step;both palms push out forward,being shoulder-width apart,hearts of palms facing forward,wrists at shoulder level.Eyes on both palms.(Fig.58)

第十一式　开合手

Form 11　Open and Close Hands

59 以右脚掌和左脚跟为轴，依次右转，两脚踏实；两掌翻转掌心相对，指尖向上，屈收至胸前，再向左右分开，与肩同宽；目视前方。

60 两掌相合，与头同宽，掌心相对；与此同时右脚跟提起成"丁"步；目视两掌中间。

◐ Using right sole and left heel as pivots,to turn right in order,both feet sit firmly;turn both palms to face each other, fingertips pointing upward,withdraw them to front of chest, then separate them out,to the side of the left and the right, being shoulder-width apart.Eyes front.(Fig.59)

◐ Close both palms,with the head-width apart,hearts of palms facing each other;while raise right heel to form a T-step.Eyes between palms.(Fig.60)

第十二式　右单鞭
Form 12　Right Single Whip

61 身体稍右转，右脚向右横开一步，脚跟着地；两臂内旋，两掌虎口相对，掌心向外；目视左掌。

62 重心右移，成右侧弓步；两掌向左右分开，平举于身体两侧，掌心转向外，掌指向上；目视左掌。

☯ The body turns slightly to right,step right foot a right side step,heel on the ground;both arms turn inward, "tiger mouth "of both palms（tiger mouth: the part of the hand between the thumb and the index finger）face each other,heart of palms facing outward.Eyes on left palm.(Fig.61)

☯ Shift weight to right,to form a right side bow step; separate both palms to the side of the left and the right, horizontally to raise to both sides of body,with hearts of palms turning outward,fingers pointing upward.Eyes on left palm. (Fig.62)

第十三式 肘底捶
Form 13 Fist Under Elbow

63 重心左移，右脚尖内扣，上体稍左转；右前臂外旋，掌心转向上，右掌向内掩裹划弧至右肩前；左掌向左、向下划弧；目视右掌。

64 重心右移，上体右转，左脚收至右脚内侧；右掌翻转屈收至右胸前，掌心向下，左前臂外旋，左掌心转向上，经腹前向右划弧，与右掌上下相对，两臂相抱如"抱球"状。

65 上体左转，左脚向左前方摆脚上一步，脚跟着地，脚尖外撇；左掌经右前臂下向上、向左划弧，掌心向内，高与头齐，右掌经左胸前划弧下落至右胯旁；目视左掌。

❀ Shift weight to left,tiptoes of right foot turned inward, the torso turns slightly to left;right forearm turns outward, with heart of palm turning upward,right palm turns inward in a curve to front of right shoulder;meanwhile,left palm moves in leftward-downward arc.Eyes on right palm.(Fig.63)

❀ Shift weight to right,the torso turns to right,withdraw left foot beside right foot;turn right palm and bend it back to the front of right chest,heart of palm facing downward, meanwhile left forearm turns outward,heart of left palm facing upward,past abdomen to right in a curve,to face right palm each other,both arms close as if embracing a ball gesture.(Fig.64)

❀ The torso turns to left,left foot takes and turns outward a step forward to left,heel on the ground,tiptoes of left foot turned outward;left palm moves past below right forearm in an upward-leftward arc,with heart of palm facing inward,at head level, meanwhile right palm moves past the front of left chest in a curve to drop down to the side of right hip.Eyes on left palm.(Fig.65)

66 上体继续左转，重心前移，右脚向前跟半步，脚前掌落在左脚后面；左臂内旋，掌心转向外，左掌向左、向下划弧至体左侧；右臂外旋，右掌向右、向前划弧至体前，高与头齐，掌心斜向上；目视前方。

67 重心移至右腿，右脚踏实，左脚向前进步，脚跟着地，脚尖上翘，成左虚步；左掌收经左腰际成侧立掌，再经右腕上向前劈出，指尖高与眉齐，右掌握拳，拳眼向上，收至左肘内侧下方；目视左掌。

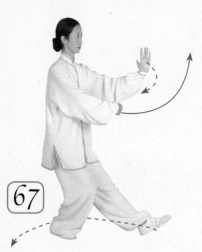

☯ Continue to turn the torso to left,shift weight forward, right foot takes half a step forward,the ball of right foot on the ground just behind left foot;left arm turns inward,heart of palm turning outward,left palm moves leftward-downward arc to left side of body;while right arm moves outward,right palm moves in a rightward-forward arc to front of body,at head level,heart of palm facing obliquely upward.Eyes front.(Fig.66)

☯ Shift weight onto right leg,set right foot firmly flat on the ground,take left foot forward,heel on the ground,tiptoes of left foot raised,to form a left empty step;left palm is withdrawn back past the part of left waist to form a side-standing palm, and over right wrist to chop forward out, fingertips at eyebrow level,while right palm is clenched into fist,eye of the fist facing upward,and withdrawn back under the inner side of left elbow. Eyes on left palm.(Fig.67)

第十四式 转身推掌
Form 14 Turn Body and Push Palm

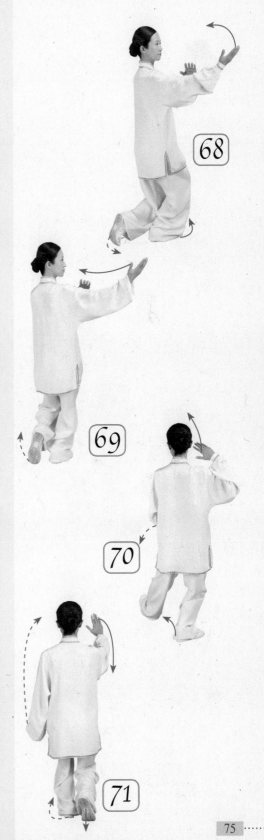

68 左脚撤至右脚后，脚前掌着地；右拳变掌上举，腕高与肩平，掌心向上；左掌翻转下落至右胸前，掌心向下；目视右掌。

69 以右脚跟、左脚掌为轴，向左转身约90°，转身时重心仍在右腿；同时右掌稍卷收，左掌稍下落；目视右掌。

70 左脚向前偏左上步，脚跟落地；右掌屈收至右耳侧，掌心斜向前下方，左掌向左划弧；目视前方。

71 重心前移，转腰顺肩，右脚收至左脚内侧后方，脚前掌着地，成右"丁"步；右掌顺势向前推出，掌心向前，指尖与鼻尖相对；左掌经左膝上搂过，按于左胯旁；目视右掌。

● Left foot takes a step backward,the ball of left foot on the ground behind right foot;open right fist to turn into a palm and raise up, wrist is at shoulder level,heart of the palm facing upward; while left palm turns downward to drop to front of right chest,heart of the palm facing downward.Eyes on right palm. (Fig.68)

● Using right heel and ball of left foot as pivots,turn to left about 90°,weight still on right leg in turning;at the same time,right palm is withdrawn back a bit,left palm drops down a little.Eyes on right palm.(Fig.69)

● Left foot takes a step forward and in slanting left direction,heel on the ground;right palm is withdrawn to side of right ear,heart of palm facing obliquely lower-front,while left palm moves leftward in an arc.Eyes front.(Fig.70)

● Shift weight forward,turn waist and shoulder followed, withdraw right foot to the inner side behind left foot,ball of right foot on the ground,forming right T-step;right palm pushes out opportunely to front,heart of palm facing forward,with fingertips facing tip of nose each other;left palm brushes over left knee and presses beside left hip. Eyes on right palm. (Fig.71)

72 以左脚跟、右脚掌为轴，向右后转身，转身后重心仍在左腿；左臂外旋向左前方上举，掌心向上，高与头平；右掌下落至左胸前，掌心向下；目视左掌。

73 右脚向前偏右上步，脚跟落地；左掌卷收至左耳侧，掌心斜向前下；右掌下落至腹前；目视前方。

74 重心前移，转腰顺肩，左脚收至右脚内侧后方，成左"丁"步；左掌顺势向前推出，掌心向前，指尖与鼻尖相对；右掌经右膝上搂过，按于右胯旁；目视左掌。

❀ Using heel of left foot and ball of right foot as pivots,turn body to rear-right,weight still on left leg;left arm turns outward to raise it up forward to left,heart of palm facing upward,at head level,while right palm drops down to front of left chest,heart of palm facing downward. Eyes on left palm.(Fig.72)

❀ Right foot takes a step toward and slanting right,heel on the ground;left palm is withdrawn to side of left ear,heart of palm facing obliquely to lower-front;while right palm drops down to front of abdomen.Eyes front.(Fig.73)

❀ Shift weight forward,turn waist and shoulder followed, withdraw left foot to the inner side behind right foot,to form left T-step;left palm pushes out opportunely to front,heart of palm facing forward,with fingertips against the tip of nose each other;right palm brushes over right knee,and presses beside right hip.Eyes on left palm.(Fig.74)

第十五式　玉女穿梭

Form 15　Fair Lady Works at Shuttles

75 上体右转，左脚向左撤半步；左臂外旋，左掌向右划弧至右胸前，掌心转向上；右掌经左前臂上方向前伸探至体前，掌心斜向下，腕高与肩平；目视右掌。

76 上体左转，重心移至左腿，右脚收至左脚内侧，脚尖点地；两掌同时自前、向下、向后捋，左掌捋至左胯旁，右掌捋至腹前；目随两手。

77 右脚向右前方上步，脚跟着地；两前臂旋转，两掌上举合于胸前，右掌心向内，指尖向左；左掌心向外，掌指附于右腕内侧；目视右掌。

❷ The torso turns to right,left foot takes half a step back to left;while left arm turns outward,left palm moves in rightward arc to front of right chest,with heart of palm turning upward;right palm extends over left forearm to front of body, heart of palm facing obliquely downward,wrist is at shoulder level.Eyes on right palm.(Fig.75)

❷ The torso turns to left,shift weight onto left leg,withdraw right foot beside left foot,tiptoes touching on the ground;both palms are stroked while from front,downward and backward,until left palm is stroked beside left hip,right palm is stroked to front of abdomen. Eyes follow both hands.(Fig.76)

❷ Right foot takes a step forward to right,heel on the ground；both forearms turn over,both palms raise up close to front of chest,heart of right palm facing inward,fingertips pointing leftward;heart of left palm facing outward, fingertips rest on the inner side of right wrist.Eyes on right palm.(Fig.77)

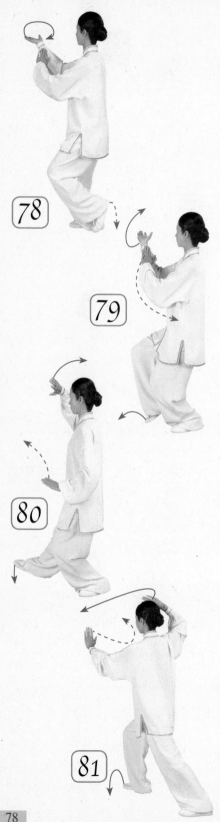

78 重心前移，上体右转，左脚随之跟至右脚内侧后方，脚前掌着地；右掌自左向前划平弧，掌心转向上；左掌随之转动；目随右掌。

79 左脚落实，上体左转，右掌屈肘内旋向右、向后划平弧；目视右掌。

80 上体右转，右脚再向右前方上一步，脚跟着地；右掌内旋翘腕至右肩前上方，掌心斜向上；左掌随之划弧后收于左腰际；目视前方。

81 重心前移，成右弓步，上体右转；右掌上架于右额前上方，掌心斜向上；左掌前按至体前，掌心向前，指尖与鼻尖相对；目视左掌。

❧ Shift weight forward,the torso turns to right,while left foot follows to the inner side behind right foot,ball of right foot on the ground;right palm moves from left to front in a horizontal curve,heart of palm turns upward;left palm following to move.Eyes follow right palm.(Fig.78)

❧ Set left foot flat on the ground,the torso turns to left,right palm and elbow bent,turns inward in a rightward-backward horizontal curve.Eyes on right palm.(Fig.79)

❧ The torso turns to right,right foot takes a step once again forward right,heel on the ground; while right palm turns inward and stands wrist to upper front of right shoulder,with heart of palm facing obliquely upward;left palm follows in a curve and then withdrawn beside left waist.Eyes front.(Fig.80)

❧ Shift weight forward to form a right bow step,the torso turns to right;right palm is held above right forehead to upper front,with heart of palm facing obliquely upward;left palm pushes forward to front of body,heart of palm facing forward, with fingertips against the tip of nose each other.Eyes on left palm.(Fig.81)

82 重心后移，右脚尖抬起内扣，上体左转；右前臂外旋，右掌翻转下落于体前，掌心向上，右腕高与肩平；左掌向右划弧后收至右肘内侧，掌心向下；目视右掌。

83 重心前移，右脚落实，上体继续左转；左掌从右前臂上穿出，并自右向左划弧抹掌；右掌收于左肘内侧下方，两掌心上下斜相对；目视左掌。

84 上体右转，左脚收至右脚内侧；两掌自前同时向下、向后捋，右掌捋至右胯旁，左掌捋至腹前；目随两掌。

85 左脚向左前方上步，脚跟着地；两前臂旋转，两掌上举合于胸前，左掌心向内，掌指向右；右掌心向外，掌指附于左腕内侧；目视左掌。

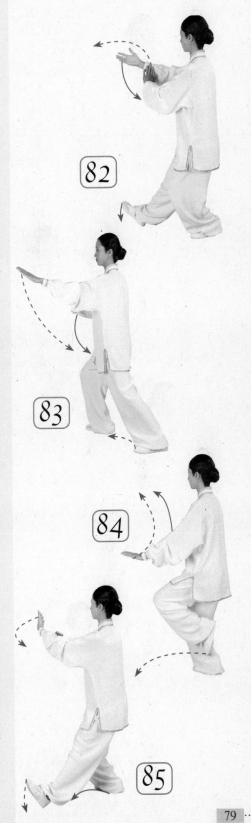

❂ Shift weight backward,tiptoes of right foot to raise and then turned inward,the torso turns to left;meanwhile right forearm turns outward,right palm turns over down to front of body,heart of palm facing upward,right wrist is at shoulder level;left palm moves to right in a curve and then withdrawn to the inner side of right elbow,heart of palm facing downward.Eyes on right palm.(Fig.82)

❂ Shift weight forward,set right foot firmly on the ground, the torso continues to turn left;while left palm threads out over right forearm,and from right to left in a curve to move rounded palms;while right palm is withdrawn to lower inside of left elbow,hearts of palms facing obliquely each other.Eyes on left palm.(Fig.83)

❂ The torso turns to right,withdraw left foot beside right foot;while both palms stroke from front,and downward-backward, until right palm strokes to the side of right hip,left palm strokes to front of abdomen.Eyes follow both palms.(Fig.84)

❂ Left foot takes a step forward to left,heel on the ground; both forearms circle until both palms raise up to close before chest,heart of left palm facing inward,fingertips pointing rightward;heart of right palm facing outward,fingertips rest on the inner side of left wrist.Eyes on left palm.(Fig.85)

86 重心前移，上体左转，右脚随之跟进至左脚内侧后方，脚前掌着地；左掌自右向前划平弧，掌心转向上，右掌随之转动；目视左掌。

87 右脚落实，上体右转，左掌屈肘内旋向左、向后划平弧；目视左掌。

88 上体左转，左脚再向左前方上一步，脚跟着地；左掌内旋翘腕至左肩前上方，掌心斜向上；右掌随之划弧后收于右腰际；目视前方。

89 重心前移，成左弓步，上体左转；左掌上架于左额前上方，掌心斜向上；右掌向前，指尖与鼻尖相对；目视右掌。

❂ Shift weight forward,the torso turns to left,while right foot follows to the inner side behind left foot,ball of right foot on the ground;left palm move from right to front in a horizontal curve,heart of palm turned upward,right palm follows to turn.Eyes on left palm.(Fig.86)

❂ Set right foot firmly on the ground,the torso turns to right, while left palm,elbow bent,turns inward in a leftward -backward horizontal curve.Eyes on left palm.(Fig.87)

❂ The torso turns to left,left foot takes a step once again forward to left,heel on the ground ;while left palm turns inward and stands wrist to upper front of left shoulder,with heart of palm facing obliquely upward;right palm follows to move a curve and then withdrawn beside right waist.Eyes front.(Fig.88)

❂ Shift weight forward to form a left bow step,the torso turns to left;while left palm is held above left forehead to upper left,with heart of palm facing obliquely upward;right palm pushes forward,fingertips against the tip of nose each other.Eyes on right palm.(Fig.89)

第十六式　右左蹬脚

Form 16　Kick with Right Heel and Left Heel

90 重心后移，左脚尖内扣，上体右转；左臂外旋，左掌翻转落于体前，掌心向上，腕高与肩平；右掌向左划弧后收至左肘内侧，掌心向下；目视左掌。

91 重心前移，上体左转；右掌从左前臂上方穿出，向上、向右划弧展开；左掌向下、向左划弧至腰侧；头随上体转动。

92 上体右转，右脚收至左脚内侧；右掌向下、向左、向上划弧；左掌向左、向上、向右划弧至胸前两腕交叠，两掌交叉合抱，右掌在外，掌心均向内；目视右前方。

● Shift weight backward,tiptoes of left foot turned inward, the torso turns to right;left arm turns outward,with palm turning down before body,heart of palm facing upward,wrist is at shoulder level;right palm moves in a leftward curve and is withdrawn to inside of left elbow,heart of palm facing downward. Eyes on left palm.(Fig.90)

● Shift weight forward,the torso turns to left;right palm threads out over left forearm,in an upward-rightward curve to expand;left palm moves in a downward-leftward curve to the side of waist.Head follows the movement of the torso.(Fig.91)

● The torso turns to right,withdraw right foot beside left foot;right palm moves in a downward-leftward-upward curve;left palm moves in a leftward-upward-rightward curve to front of chest,across both wrists,with both palms cross to close,right palm in front of the left, hearts of palms completely inward.Eyes toward front-right.(Fig.92)

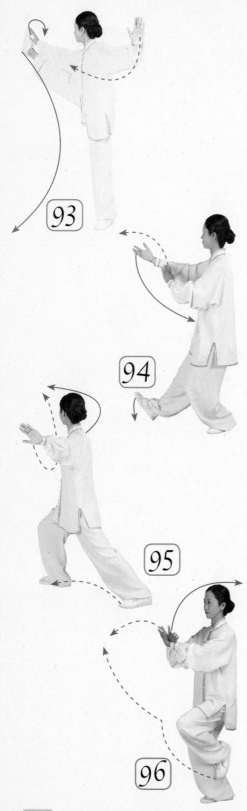

93 左腿微屈站稳，右腿屈膝提起，右脚向右前方（约30°）慢慢蹬出，脚尖上勾，脚跟高过腰部；两掌分别向右前方和左方划弧分开，掌心向外，腕与肩平，两臂伸展，肘微屈，右臂与右腿上下相对；目视右掌。

94 右腿屈收，右脚向右前方落下，脚跟着地；右前臂外旋，右掌心转向上，稍向内收；左掌下落，经腰间向前、向上划弧伸至右肘内侧，掌心向下；目视右掌。

95 重心前移，右脚落实，上体右转；左掌从右前臂上方穿出向上、向左划弧展开；右掌向下、向右划弧至腰侧；头随上体转动。

96 上体左转，左脚收至右脚内侧；左右两掌分别向外划弧，至胸前两腕交叠，两掌交叉合抱，左掌在外，掌心均向内；目视左前方。

❀ Left leg bent slightly stands firmly,right leg is bent at knee to lift up,kick with right foot slowly towards front-right direction(about 30°),with tiptoes upturned ,the heel is over the part of the waist;separate both palms in a forward-right and left curve,both hearts of palms turning outward,wrists are at shoulder level,and extend both arms, elbows are slightly bent,right arm is in vertical line with right leg.Eyes on right palm.(Fig.93)

❀ Right leg is bent and withdrawn,right foot drops down towards forward-right direction,heel on the ground;while right forearm turns outward,heart of right palm turns upward and withdrawn back slightly;left palm drops down past the part of waist, in a forward-upward curve to extend to the inside of right elbow, heart of palm facing downward.Eyes on right palm.(Fig.94)

❀ Shift weight forward,set right foot firmly on the ground, the torso turns to right;left palm threads out over right forearm in an upward-leftward curve to open out,right palm moves in a downward-rightward curve to the side of waist.Head follows the movement of the torso.(Fig.95)

❀ The torso turns to left,withdraw left foot beside right foot;left palm moves in a downward-rightward-upward curve, right palm moves in a rightward-upward-leftward curve to front of chest across both wrists,with both palms cross to close,left palm is in front of the right,hearts of palms are completely inward. Eyes toward front-left.(Fig.96)

97 右腿微屈站稳，左腿屈膝提起，左脚向左前方（约30°）慢慢蹬出，脚尖上勾，脚跟高过腰部；两掌分别向左前方和右方划弧分开，掌心向外，腕与肩平，两臂伸展，肘微屈，左臂与左腿上下相对；目视左掌。

☯ Right leg bent slightly stands firmly,left leg bent at knee to lift up,kick with left foot slowly forward to left direction(about 30°),with tiptoes upturned,the heel is over the part of the waist;separate both palms in a front-left and right curve,both hearts of palms turning outward,wrists are at shoulder level,and extend both arms, elbows are slightly bent,left arm is in vertical line with left leg.Eyes on left palm.(Fig.97)

第十七式　掩手肱捶
Form 17　Strike with Hidden Fist

98 左小腿屈收，左脚落于右脚内侧，两臂外旋，两掌掩合于头前，与头同宽，掌心向内；目视两掌。

99 左脚尖上翘，脚跟擦地向左开步，上体稍右转；两臂内旋，两掌翻转下落，上下交叉相叠于小腹右侧，左掌压于右掌背上，掌心均向下；目视前方。

☯ Bend and withdraw left lower leg inward,left foot drops down beside right foot,both arms turn outward,with both palms come close together before face,with head-width,hearts of palms facing inward.Eyes on both palms.(Fig.98)

☯ Raised tiptoes of left foot,the heel of left foot rubs ground to take a step to left,the torso turns to right slightly;both arms turn inward,palms turn down,pile left palm on the back of right palm to press down to right side of abdomen,hearts of palms facing completely downward.Eyes front.(Fig.99)

100 上体转正，重心左移于两腿之间；两掌向两侧分开，高与肩平，前臂内旋，掌心转向外；目视前方。

101 重心右移，上体微右转；两臂外旋，肘内合，左掌摆至体前，掌心向上，高与肩平；右掌变拳，屈臂合于胸前，拳心向上；目视左掌。

102 重心左移，上体左转，转腰顺肩，成左弓步；右拳旋转向前方冲打，拳心转向下；左掌后收，掌心贴于左腹部，指尖向右；目视右拳。

☯ The torso turns straight,shift weight between both legs; while separate both palms to both sides,at shoulder level, forearms turn inward,with hearts of palms turning outward.Eyes front.(Fig.100)

☯ Shift weight to right,the torso turns slightly to right; both arms turn outward,both elbows are turned inward about,left palm swings to front of the body,heart of the palm turning upward,at shoulder level;while right palm turns into a fist, bend the arm to close before chest,heart of fist facing upward. Eyes on left palm.(Fig.101)

☯ Shift weight to left,the torso turns to left,turn waist and shoulder followed ,to form a left bow step;right fist turns to strike out forward in a straight blow,heart of fist turning downward;left palm is withdraw backward,heart of the palm rests on a part of left abdomen,fingertips pointing right.Eyes on right fist.(Fig.102)

第十八式 野马分鬃

Form 18　Part the Wild Horse's Mane

103 上体左转；右拳变掌向下划弧至腹前，掌心向下；左掌以拇指为轴，四指顺时针向下转动。

104 重心右移，上体右转，右臂内旋，右掌翻转向外，并向上、向右划弧，屈臂置于右肩前，拇指向下，四指尖向左；左臂外旋，掌心转向内，掌指背贴于右前臂内侧，随之划弧，两臂撑圆；目视右掌。

105 重心左移，上体左转；右臂外旋，左臂内旋，两掌成横掌，掌心向左前方，横捌于腹前，腰腹弹性发力；目视两掌。

❷ The torso turns to left;open right fist to palm in a downward curve to front of abdomen,heart of palm facing downward;using the thumb of left palm as pivot,turning four fingers downward in the same direction as clockwise.(Fig.103)

❷ Shift weight to right,the torso turns to right,right arm turns inward,right palm turns outward and moves in an upward-rightward curve and bend right arm to front of right shoulder,the thumb facing downward,four fingertips pointing leftward;left arm turns outward,with heart of palm turning inward,back of left fingers rests on the inside of right forearm and following right forearm to circle,both arms are rounded. Eyes on right palm.(Fig.104)

❷ Shift weight to left,the torso turns to left;right arm turns outward,left arm turns inward,both palms form two sideways palms,hearts of palms facing forward to left and horizontal to fend before abdomen,to apply force which is explosive from waist and abdomen.Eyes on both palms. (Figs.105A, 105B)

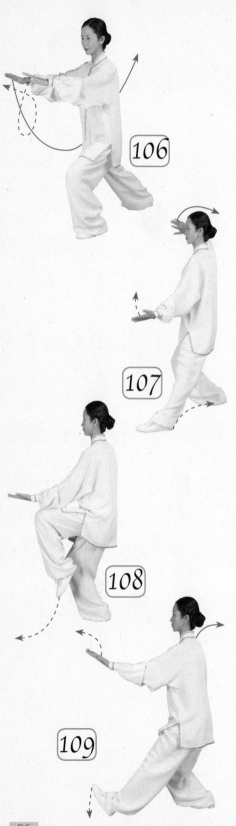

106 腰与腹放松折叠回旋，再向左转；两掌自右向左划弧，皆成俯掌，交错摆至胸前，左掌略在前；眼看左掌。

107 重心右移，腰向右转，两掌向右划弧分开，左掌心转向上，右掌心转向右；目视前方。

108 重心后移，左脚屈膝提起；左臂外旋，左掌向上托于左膝上方；右掌向右上划弧横于体右侧，掌心向外，高与肩平；目视前方。

109 左脚向前上步；目视前方。

❀ The waist and abdomen are relaxed and fold to turn in an arc,turn to left once again;both palms turn from right to left in a curve,palms completely facing down and crisscross swing to front chest,left palm slightly forward. Eyes on left palm.(Fig.106)

❀ Shift weight to right,waist turns to right,both palms turn towards right in a curve to open, heart of left palm turns upward, heart of right palm turning rightward.Eyes front.(Fig.107)

❀ Shift weight backward,lift left foot with knee bent;left arm turns outward,with palm holding upward above left knee; right palm moves in an upper-right curve across to right side of body,heart of palm facing outward at shoulder level. Eyes front.(Fig.108)

❀ Left foot takes a step forward.Eyes front.(Fig.109)

110 重心前移，成左弓步；左掌向前穿靠，掌心向上，指尖向前，左腕高与肩平；右掌撑至身体右方，掌心向外，指尖斜向上，腕高与肩平；目视左掌。

111 重心后移，左脚尖外撇，上体左转，左臂内旋，左掌心翻转向外，并稍屈臂外撑；右臂亦外旋，右掌稍下落内收；目视左掌。

112 重心前移，上体左转，右脚屈膝向前提起；右掌向下划弧，经体侧前举，托于右膝上方，掌心向上；左掌左摆横于体侧，掌心向外，指尖斜向上；目视右掌。

113 右脚向前上步；目视前方。

❂ Shift weight forward to form a left bow step;left palm threads and extends forward,heart of palm facing upward, fingertips pointing forward,left wrist is at shoulder level; right palm is rounded to right direction of body,heart of palm facing outward,fingertips facing obliquely upward,wrist is at shoulder level.Eyes on left palm.(Fig.110)

❂ Shift weight backward,tiptoes of left foot turns outward, the torso turns to left,left arm turns inward,heart of left palm turns outward,and left arm is bent a bit to rounds out;while right arm also turns outward,right palm slightly drops down and withdraw inward.Eyes on left palm.(Fig.111)

❂ Shift weight forward,the torso turns to left,right foot with knee bent raises forward up;right palm moves in a downward curve,past the side of body,hold the palm over right knee,heart of palm facing upward;left palm swing to left across to side of body,heart of palm facing outward,fingertips pointing obliquely upward.Eyes on right palm.(Fig.112)

❂ Right foot takes a step forward.Eyes front.(Fig.113)

114 重心前移，成右弓步，右掌向前穿靠，掌心向上，指尖向前，腕高与肩平；左掌撑至身体左方，掌心向外，指尖斜向上，腕高与肩平；目视右掌。

☯ Shift weight forward to form a right bow step,right palm threads and extends forward,heart of palm facing upward, fingertips pointing forward,wrist is at shoulder level left palm rounds to left direction of body,heart of palm facing outward,fingertips facing obliquely upward,wrist is at shoulder level.Eyes on right palm.(Fig.114)

第十九式　云手

Form 19　Wave Hands Like Clouds on Both Sides

115 重心左移，右脚尖内扣，上体左转；右前臂内旋，右掌塌腕右旋，向左摆至右肩前；左掌微向左撑，掌心向左；目视右掌。

116 重心右移，上体右转，左脚跟随之碾动；右掌翻转向外，横掌右摆至身体右侧；左掌自左向下，经腹前向右划弧，掌心随之翻转向上；目随右掌。

☯ Shift weight to left,tiptoes of right foot turns inward,the torso turns to left;right forearm turns inward,right palm with wrist relaxed turns to right,and swings towards left to the front of right shoulder;prop left palm towards left a little, heart of palm facing leftward.Eyes on right palm.(Fig.115)

☯ Shift weight to right,the torso turns right,heel of left foot follows to move;right palm turns outward,swing to right in horizontal palm to right side of body;while left palm moves from left and downward,past the front of abdomen in a rightward curve,with heart of palm turning upward.Eyes follow the movement of right palm.(Fig.116)

117 重心左移，上体左转；左掌掌心向内，自右向上向左，经面前划弧云转，指尖与眉同高；右掌向下经腹前，向左划弧云转，掌心由外转向内；目随右掌。

118 上体继续左转，右脚收于左脚内侧落地，两脚平行脚尖向前，相距10～20厘米；两掌云至身体左侧逐渐翻转，左掌心转向外，右掌云至左肘内侧，掌心转向内；目视左掌。

119 重心右移，上体右转；右掌自左经面前向右划弧云转，指尖高与眉齐；左掌向下经腹前向右划弧云转；目视右掌。

120 上体继续右转，左脚向左侧开步，脚尖仍向前；两掌云至身体右侧，逐渐翻转，右掌心转向外，左掌云至右肘内侧，掌心转向内；目视右掌。

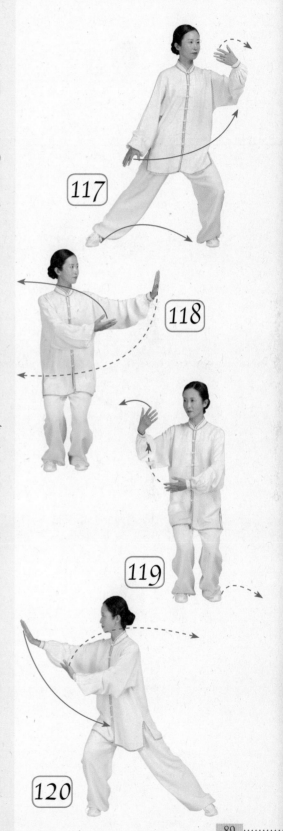

❧ Shift weight to left,the torso turns to left;heart of left palm moves inward,from right to upward-leftward direction,past face in a wave curve to turn,with fingertips at eyebrow level;right palm moves downward past the front of abdomen,in a leftward wave curve to turn,with heart of the palm from out turning inward. Eyes follow the movement of right palm.(Fig.117)

❧ The torso continues to turn to left,bring right foot parallel to the side of the left foot and flat on the ground,tiptoes of both feet pointing forward and both feet 10～20cm apart;both palms move in a wave circle to left side of body and then turned over,heart of left palm turning outward,right palm moving in a wave circle to inside of left elbow,with heart of palm turning inward. Eyes on left palm. (Fig.118)

❧ Shift weight to right,the torso turns to right;right palm moves from left past face towards right in a wave circle to turn,the fingertips at eyebrow level;while left palm moves downward past front of abdomen towards right in a wave circle to turn.Eyes on right palm.(Fig.119)

❧ The torso continues to turn to right,left foot takes a side step to left,with tiptoes still pointing forward;both palms move in a wave arc to right side of the body and gradually turn over,heart of right palm turning outward,left palm to the inside of right elbow,with heart of palm turning inward.Eyes on right palm.(Fig.120)

121 重心左移，上体左转；左掌经面前向左划弧云转；右掌向下经腹前划弧向左云转；目随左掌。

122 上体继续左转，右脚收于左脚内侧落地，两脚平行脚尖向前，相距10～20厘米；两掌云至身体左侧逐渐翻转，左掌心转向外，右掌云至左肘内侧，掌心转向内；目视左掌。

123 重心右移，上体右转；右掌自左经面前向右划弧云转，指尖高与眉齐；左掌向下经腹前向右划弧云转；目视右掌。

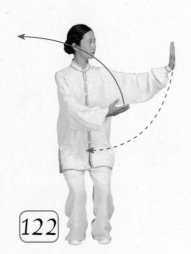

● Shift weight to left,the torso turns to left;left palm moves past face towards left in a wave curve to turn;while right palm moves downward past the front of abdomen towards left in a wave curve to turn.Eyes follow the movement of left palm. (Fig.121)

● The torso continues to turn to left,bring right foot parallel to the side of left foot and flat on the ground,tiptoes of both feet pointing forward,both feet within 10～20cm apart;both palms move in a wave circle to turn to left side of the body,and then gradually turned over,heart of left palm turning outward,right palm moving to inside of left elbow,with heart of palm turning inward.Eyes on left palm.(Fig.122)

● Shift weight to right,the torso turns to right;right palm from left past face moves towards right in a wave curve to turn,with fingertips at eyebrow level;while left palm moves down past the front of abdomen towards right in a wave curve to turn.Eyes on right palm.(Fig.123)

124 上体继续右转，左脚向左侧开步，脚尖仍向前；两掌云至身体右侧，逐渐翻转，右掌心转向外，左掌云至右肘内侧，掌心转向内；目视右掌。

125 重心左移，上体左转；左掌经面前向左划弧云转；右掌向下经腹前划弧向左云转；目随左掌。

126 上体继续左转，右脚收于左脚内侧落地，脚尖内扣约45°落地，相距10～20厘米；两掌云至身体左侧逐渐翻转，左掌心转向外，右掌云至左肘内侧，掌心转向内；目视左掌。

☯ The torso continues to turn to right,left foot takes a side step to left,with tiptoes still pointing forward;both palms move in arc to right side of the body,and gradually turn over,heart of right palm turning outward,left palm to the inside of right elbow,with heart of palm turning inward.Eyes on right palm.(Fig.124)

☯ Shift weight to left,the torso turns to left;left palm moves past face in a leftward curve while right palm moves downward past the front of abdomen in a leftward curve.Eyes follow the movement of left palm.(Fig.125)

☯ The torso continues to turn to left,bring right foot to the side of left foot and flat on the ground,tiptoes of it turn inward about 45°and flat on the ground,both feet within 10～20cm apart;both palms move in a wave circle to left side of the body and gradually turned over,heart of left palm turning outward,right palm moves in a wave circle to the inside of left elbow,with heart of palm turning inward.Eyes on left palm. (Fig.126)

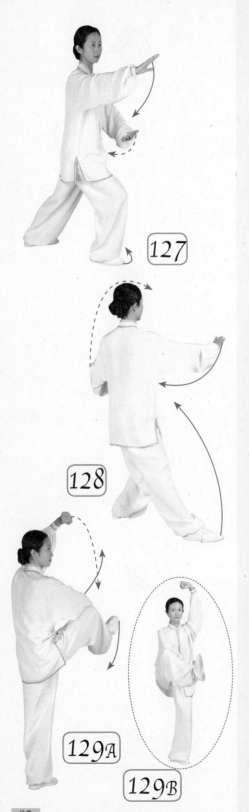

127

128

129A

129B

第二十式　独立打虎
Form 20　Hit the Tiger on One Leg

127 重心右移，左脚向身后撤一步，右腿屈膝前弓；左掌掌心翻转向上，向下划弧，收于腹前；右掌掌心翻转向下，经左前臂上方穿出，向前伸探至体前，腕高与肩平；目视右掌。

128 重心左移，上体左转，右脚尖内扣；两掌向下，经腹前向左划弧；视线随上体转动。

129 两掌逐渐握拳，左拳经体侧屈臂上举至左额前上方，拳心向外，拳眼斜向下；右拳屈臂收于左胸前，拳心向内，拳眼向上；左腿微屈站稳，右腿屈膝提起，右脚收至裆前，脚尖上翘，头转向右前方；目平视前方。

❀ Shift weight to right,left foot take a step backward,bend right knee to bow forward;while heart of left palm turns upward,to move downward in an arc,and withdraws it to the front of abdomen; heart of right palm turns downward past upper of left forearm to thread out,extending to the front of body,wrist is at shoulder level.Eyes on right palm.(Fig.127)

❀ Shift weight to left,the torso turns to left,tiptoes of right foot turn inward;both palms turn downward,past the front of abdomen in a curve towards left.Eyes follow the movement of the torso.(Fig.128)

❀ Clench gradually both palms into fists,left fist past the side of the body,with arm bent,raises up to the upper-front of left forehead,heart of the fist facing upward,eye of the fist facing obliquely downward; right fist,with arm bent,withdrawn to front of left chest,heart of fist facing inward, eye of the fist facing upward;left leg bent slightly stands firmly,right leg,with knee bent,lifts up,right foot is withdrawn to front of crotch,tiptoes of right foot raised,head turning forward to right.Eyes looking straight forward. (Figs.129A, 129B)

第二十一式 右分脚

Form 21 Separation of Right Foot

130 上体微右转，右脚内收，脚尖下垂；两拳变掌叠抱于胸前，右掌在外，掌心皆向内；目视右前方。

131 右脚脚面展平，脚尖向右前方慢慢踢出，高过腰部；两掌同时向右前方和左方划弧分开，掌心皆向外，指尖向上，腕高与肩平，两臂撑举，肘关节微屈，右臂与右腿上下相对；目视右掌。

☯ The torso turns slightly to right,right foot is withdrawn inward,tiptoes of right foot hanging downward;both fists turn into palms cross before chest,right palm is out,both hearts of palms completely inward.Eyes forward to right.(Fig.130)

☯ The instep of right foot stretches flat,kick out with tiptoes of right foot slowly towards front-right,over the waist;at the same time,both palms separate towards front-right and to left in a curve,hearts of palms facing completely outward, fingertips pointing upward,wrists are at shoulder level,both arms extending and raising,joints of elbow bent slightly ,right arm is in vertical line with right leg.Eyes on right palm. (Fig.131)

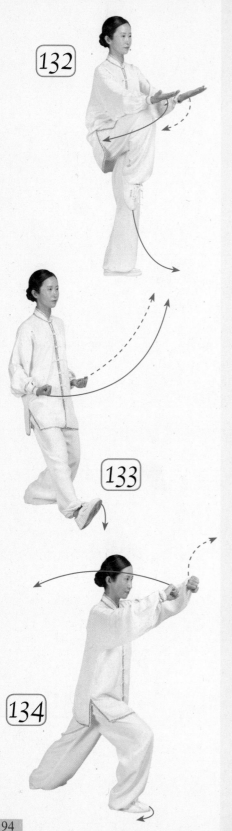

第二十二式　双峰贯耳
Form 22　Strike Opponent's Ears with Both Fists

132 右腿屈膝，小腿回收，脚尖下垂；两臂屈肘外旋，在胸前相合，两掌经面前划弧平行下落于右膝上方，掌心翻向上；目视前方。

133 右脚向前落步，脚跟着地；两掌分落于腰侧，逐渐握拳，拳心向上；目视前方。

134 重心前移，成右弓步；两拳同时经两侧向前上方划弧贯打，高与耳齐，相距同头宽，拳眼斜向下，两臂半屈成钳形；目视前方。

❀ Right leg is bent at knee,the lower leg is withdrawn,with tiptoes of right foot pointing naturally downward;both arms are bent at elbows to turn outward,and to close before chest,both palms past face in an even curve,drop down above right knee, hearts of palms turned upward.Eyes front.(Fig.132)

❀ Take right foot down to front,heel on the ground;while palms drop to both sides of hips,clench palms gradually into fists,hearts of them facing upward.Eyes front.(Fig.133)

❀ Shift weight forward to form a right bow step;while both fists past both sides towards the upper front move an arc to strike,at ear level,with head-width apart,eyes of fists facing obliquely downward,both arms semi-bent in a pincer movement. Eyes front.(Fig.134)

第二十三式 左分脚

Form 23　Separation of Left Foot

135 重心后移，右脚尖外撇，上体右转；两拳变掌左右分开，掌心皆向外，目视左掌。

136 重心前移，左脚收于右脚内侧，上体微左转；两掌从左右两侧向下、向内划弧，至腹前相交，举抱于胸前，左掌在外，掌心皆向内；目视左前方。

137 右腿微屈站稳，左腿屈膝提起，左脚尖向左前上方（与起势方向成90°）慢慢踢出，脚面展平，高过腰部；两掌向左前方和右方划弧分开，掌心向外，腕与肩平，两臂撑举，肘关节微屈，左臂与左腿上下相对；目视左掌。

● Shift weight backward,tiptoes of right foot turns outward, the torso turns to right;open both fists to palms to separate the side of the left and the right,hearts of palms completely facing outward.Eyes on left palm.(Fig.135)

● Shift weight forward,withdraw left foot beside right foot, the torso turns to left slightly;both palms move from both sides of the left and the right in a downward-inward curve,until they cross in front of abdomen,and then up to the front of chest,left palm in front of right palm,both palms completely inward.Eyes front-left.(Fig.136)

● Right leg is bent at knee slightly and stands firmly,left leg with knee bent raises up,tiptoes of left foot gradually kicks out towards to upper front to left(make a 90° angle according to the direction of starting posture),with the instep stretched flat, over the waist;both palms separate to front-left side and right side in a curve,hearts of palms facing outward,wrists at shoulder level,and both arms stretch to raise up,elbows slightly bent,and left arm is in vertical line with left leg.Eyes on left palm.(Fig.137)

第二十四式　转身拍脚
Form 24　Turn Body and Slap Foot

138 左腿屈收下落，身体以右脚掌为轴顺势向右后转身，左脚尖随体转内扣落地，两掌从两侧向腹前划弧下落，两前臂外旋，掌心斜相对；头随身体转动。

139 重心左移，身体继续右后转（侧对上势左分脚方向），右脚随之转正，脚尖点地；两掌交叉，右掌在外举抱于胸前；目视右前方。

140 左腿支撑，右脚向上踢摆，脚面展平；两前臂内旋，掌心转向外，右掌向前击拍右脚面，高与头齐，左掌向后划弧分开，平举于身体左方，腕高与肩平；目视右掌。

◐ Left leg is withdrawn back and drops down,the body uses the ball of right foot as pivot,opportunely turns back to right, tiptoes of left foot follow the body to turn inward and drop down on the ground,both palms drop down from both sides to front of abdomen in an arc,both forearms turn outward,hearts of palms facing obliquely each other.Head following movement of body. (Fig.138)

◐ Shift weight to left,body continues to turn to rear-right (side opposite the direction of separation of left foot),with right foot following and then turning straight,tiptoes of right foot touching on the ground;both palms cross,right palm in front of left palm up to the front of chest.Eyes toward front-right. (Fig.139)

◐ Stand on left leg,right foot kicks upward,with instep stretched flat;both forearms turn inward,hearts of palms turn outward,right palm slaps forward on right instep,to head level, separate left palm backward in an arc and horizontally raises to left side of body,wrist at shoulder level.Eyes on right palm.(Fig.140)

第二十五式 进步栽捶

Form 25　Step Up and Punch Downward

141 左腿屈膝，右腿屈收，右脚前落，脚尖外撇，上体右转，重心前移；两前臂外旋，左掌向上、向右划弧，掌心转向右；右掌翻转下落至腰间，掌心向上；头随上体转动。

142 上体继续右转，左脚收至右脚内侧；右掌继续自下而上划弧至右后方，左掌经头前划弧至右肋；目视右掌。

143 左脚向前上一步，脚跟着地，上体微左转；右掌向右、向上划弧，屈肘握拳收于右耳侧，拳心向下，左掌向下划弧落于腹前；目视前下方。

144 上体左转，稍向前俯身，重心前移，成左弓步；右拳向前下方打出，高与腹平，拳面向前下方，拳眼向左；左掌自左膝上方搂过，按于左胯旁；目视右拳。

❂ Bend left leg at knee,right leg is withdrawn in,right foot drops forward,tiptoes of right foot turned outward,the torso turns to right,shift weight forward;both forearms turn outward, left palm moves in an upward-rightward curve,heart of palm turning rightward;right palm turns over to drop down to part of the waist,heart of palm facing upward.Head following the movement of body.(Fig.141)

❂ The torso turn to right still,withdraw left foot beside right foot;right palm goes on moving from down place to up place in a curve to the rear-right,left palm moves an arc past head to right ribs.Eyes on right palm.(Fig.142)

❂ Left foot takes a step forward,the heel on the ground,the torso turns to left slightly;right palm moves in a rightward-upward curve to bend elbow and clench it into a fist close to side of right ear,heart of fist facing downward,left palm moves in a downward curve to front of abdomen.Eyes toward front and down. (Fig.143)

❂ The torso turns to left,slightly bend trunk forward,shift weight forward,to form a left bow step;right fist punches to lower-front,at abdomen level,the face of fist facing lower-forward,with eye of fist facing leftward;left palm brushes over left knee to press beside left hip.Eyes on right fist.(Fig.144)

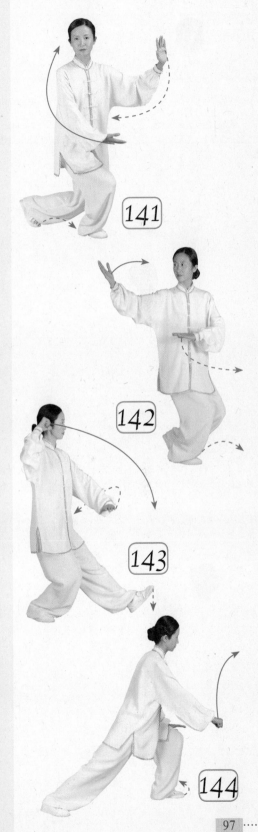

141

142

143

144

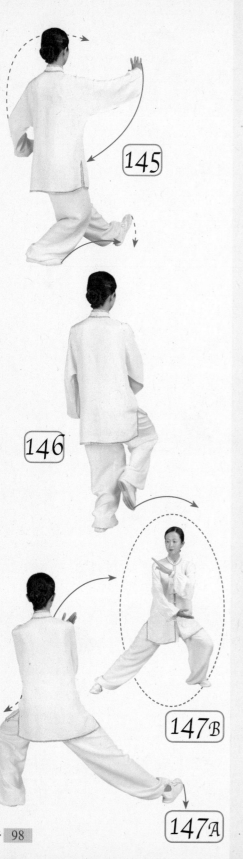

第二十六式　斜飞势
Form 26　Slant Flying

145 重心后移，左脚尖外撇，上体左转，右拳变掌向上、向右划弧，左掌向左划弧，两掌分开。

146 右脚收于左脚内侧；左掌向上、向右划弧，屈臂于胸前，掌心斜向下；右掌向下、向左划弧，屈臂于腹前，掌心斜向上；两臂交叉相抱，左前臂在上；目视左掌。

147 上体微右转，右脚向右侧开步，脚跟着地；目视左掌。

☯ Shift weight backward,tiptoes of left foot turned outward, the torso turns to left,open right fist to palm and moves in an upward-rightward arc,left palm in a curve towards left, separate both palms.(Fig.145)

☯ Right foot is withdrawn beside the left foot;left palm moves in an upward-rightward curve,to bend the arm to front of chest,with heart of palm facing obliquely downward;right palm moves in a downward-leftward curve,to bend arm to front of abdomen,with heart of palm facing obliquely upward;both arms are closed and left forearm is up.Eyes on left palm.(Fig.146)

☯ Shift weight to right slightly,right foot takes a side step to right,heel on the ground.Eyes on left palm.(Figs.147A, 147B)

148 重心右移，成右侧弓步，右肩向右倾靠；两掌分别撑开；右掌略高于头，左掌与胯同高；目随左掌。

☯ Shift weight to right,form a right-side bow step,right shoulder tilts to strike rightward;both palms are separated to prop on both sides,right palm is slightly higher than head,left palm is high as left hip,Eyes following left palm. (Figs.148A, 148B)

第二十七式　单鞭下势
Form 27　Single Whip and Push Down

149 重心左移，右脚跟稍外展；左掌变勾手，提至身体左侧，腕与肩同高；右掌向左划弧，经头前摆至左肘内侧；目随右掌。

150 左腿全蹲，成右仆步；右掌下落经腹前顺右腿内侧向右穿出，目视右掌。

☯ Shift weight to left,the heel of right foot pointing outward slightly;left palm turns into hooked hand and raises up to left side of body,wrist is high as shoulder;right palm moves in an arc to left,past head to swing to inside of left elbow.Eyes follow right palm.(Fig.149)

☯ Left leg crouches fully,to form a right crouching step;right palm drops down past abdomen along the inner side of right leg to thread out.Eyes follow right palm.(Figs.150A, 150B)

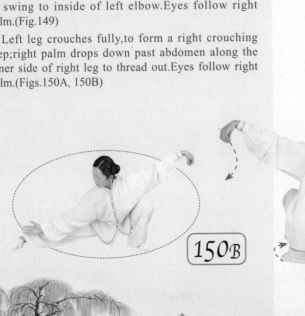

第二十八式　金鸡独立
Form 28　Golden Cock Stands on One Leg

151 重心右移，上体右转，右脚尖外展，左脚尖内扣，右腿屈弓，左腿自然蹬直；右掌向上挑至体前，成侧立掌，腕高与肩平；左臂内旋下落至身后，勾尖向上；目视右掌。

152 重心前移，上体右转，左腿屈膝向前上提起，脚尖下垂；右腿微屈站稳，成右独立步；左勾手变掌，经体侧向前、向上挑起，成侧立掌，指尖高与眉齐；右掌翻转下按于右胯旁；目视左掌。

153 右腿稍屈，左脚落于右脚内侧后方，重心后移；左掌翻转下落，右掌向下伸展。

🌒 Shift weight to right,the torso turns to right,tiptoes of right foot turns outward,and tiptoes of left foot turns inward,bend right leg at knee to bow,straighten left leg naturally;snap right palm upward to front of body,form a side-standing palm,the wrist is at shoulder level,left arm turns inward and then drops down behind body,with tip of left hooked hand facing upward.Eyes on right palm.(Fig.151)

🌒 Shift weight forward,the torso turns to right,bend left leg at knee to raise up forward,tiptoes of left foot hanging down; right leg bent a bit stands on the ground firmly to form a right independent step;open left hooked hand into a palm,and then snap it up,past the side of body,forward-upward,to form a side-standing palm,with fingertips at the same level to the eyebrow; while right palm turns down to press beside right hip.Eyes on left palm.(Fig.152)

🌒 Bend right leg slightly,left foot drops to the inner behind right foot,shift weight backward;left palm turns down,while right palm extends downward.(Fig.153)

154 上体左转，右腿屈膝提起，脚尖下垂，左腿微屈站稳，成左独立步；左掌按于左胯旁；右掌成侧立掌挑至体前，指尖高与眉齐；目视右掌。

The torso turns to left,bend right leg at knee to raise up,tiptoes of right foot hanging downward,left leg bent a bit stands on the ground firmly to form a left independent step;left palm presses beside left hip;while snap right palm to the front of body,to form a side-standing palm,with fingertips at the same level to the eyebrow. Eyes on right palm.(Fig.154)

第二十九式　退步穿掌
Form 29　Step Back and Thread Palm

155 左腿稍屈，右脚下落于左脚内侧；右掌伸于体前，左掌上提于左肋旁；目视前方。

156 右脚后撤一步；右腿自然蹬直，左腿屈弓，左脚以前脚掌为轴顺势扭正，成左弓步；左臂外旋，左掌翻转掌心向上，收经腰间，从右前臂上穿出，腕高与肩平；右臂内旋，横掌下按，落于左肘下方；目视左掌。

Bend left leg slightly,right foot drops to the inner side of left foot;right palm stretches to front of body,left palm raises up to the side of left ribs.Eyes front.(Fig.155)

Right foot takes a step backward;right leg straighten naturally, bend left leg at knee,left foot turns opportunely straight at pivot on the ball of left foot,to form a left bow step;left arm turns outward,with palm turning upward,and pulls it past the part of waist,to thread its way out over right forearm,the wrist at shoulder level;right arm turns inward,form a sweeping palm to press down below left elbow.Eyes on left palm.(Fig.156)

第三十式　虚步压掌

Form 30　Press Down Palms on Empty Step

157 重心后移，左脚尖内扣，上体右后转；右掌收至腹前，左掌举于左额侧上方；目随转体平视。

158 重心移至左腿，右脚提起，脚尖转向前方，脚前掌落地，成右虚步；上体向下松沉，微向前俯；左掌自上而下横按于右膝前上方，指尖向右；右掌按于右胯旁，指尖向前；目视前下方。

❷ Shift weight backward,tiptoes of left foot turned inward, the torso turns to the rear-right,withdraw right palm to front of abdomen and raise left palm up above sideways left forehead.Eyes follow the movement of the body and straight forward.(Fig.157)

❷ Shift weight on left leg,right foot raises up,with tiptoes turning forward and ball on the ground,to form a right empty step;the torso is relaxed and sinking,and leaning a bit forward;left palm from top to bottom,sweeps and presses above right knee to upper front,with fingertips pointing right;while right palm presses down beside right hip,with fingertips pointing forward.Eyes lower-front.(Figs.158A, 158B)

第三十一式　独立托掌

Form 31　Stand on One Leg and Hold out Palm

159 左脚蹬地；左腿微屈站稳，右腿屈膝提起，脚尖下垂，成左独立步；右掌翻转上托，举于体前，掌心向上，腕高与胸平；左掌向左、向上划弧，撑于体侧，腕高与肩平，掌心向外，指尖斜向上；目视右掌。

❷ Left foot sets firmly on the ground,left leg is slightly bent at knee to stand firmly,right leg is bent at knee to raise up, tiptoes of right foot pointing downward,to form a left independent step;turn right palm over and hold it up,to raise before the body,heart of palm facing upward,wrist at chest level;while left palm moves in a leftward-upward curve,to prop up on the side of the body,wrist at shoulder level,heart of palm facing outward,with fingertips pointing obliquely upward.Eyes on right palm.(Fig.159)

第三十二式　马步靠

Form 32　Push Forearm on Horse-riding Step

160 右脚前落，脚尖外撇，重心前移，上体右转；右臂内旋，右掌翻转下捋；左臂外旋，左掌向上、向右划弧；目视前方。

161 左脚收于右脚内侧，上体继续右转；右掌翻转向上，并向右划弧举于体侧，高与头平；左掌握拳，落于右腹前，拳心向下，拳眼向内；目视右掌。

162 上体左转，左脚向左前方上步，左臂内旋，摆至身体左侧。

163 重心略向前移，成半马步；左臂内旋，向前靠出，左拳拳眼向内，拳面向下，置于左膝前；右掌屈收，经身侧推助左臂向前挤靠，拳心向左，掌指附于左上臂内侧；目视左前方。

❧ Right foot drops down to front,tiptoes of right foot turned outward,shift weight forward,the torso turns to right;right arm turns inward,with palm turning down to stroke;left arm turns outward,left palm moves in an upward-rightward curve. Eyes front.(Fig.160)

❧ Withdraw left foot beside right foot,the torso continues to turn to right;right palm is turned upward and then moves in a rightward curve to raise to the side of the body,at head level;left palm is clenched into a fist and drops it to front of abdomen,with heart of fist facing downward,eye of fist facing inward.Eyes on right palm.(Fig.161)

❧ The torso turns to left,left foot takes a step forward to left,left arm turns inward,swing it to left side of the body. (Fig.162)

❧ Shift weight forward a bit,to form a half horse-riding step; left arm turns inward,to push forward,eye of left fist turned inward,face of left fist facing downward,place before left knee; right palm is withdrawn inward,past the side of the body to help left arm pressing and striking forward,heart of fist facing leftward, with fingers resting on inside of left arm.Eyes front-left.(Fig.163)

第三十三式　转身大捋
Form 33　Turn Body with Big Stroke

164 重心后移，左脚尖外撇抬起；左拳变掌，左臂外旋，右臂内旋，两掌心同时转向外，并微向后收带；目视两掌。

165 上体左转，重心前移，右脚收于左脚内侧，两脚平行向前，重心仍偏于左腿，并稍向上升高；左臂内旋，左掌屈肘提至胸前，横掌掌心向外；右臂外旋，举于身体右侧，高与肩平，掌心向上；目视右掌。

166 右脚前掌为轴，脚跟外展，身体左转，两掌随转身向左平捋至体前。

☯ Shift weight backward,tiptoes of left foot raised and turned outward;open left fist into a palm,left arm turns outward,right arm turns inward,while hearts of palms turn outward and withdraw them a bit backward.Eyes on both palms. (Fig.164)

☯ The torso turns to left,shift weight forward;withdraw right foot beside left foot,both feet are parallel each other forward,with bulk of weight still on left leg,and then stand upward slightly;left arm turns inward,left palm and benting elbow, raises up before chest,and the palm turning into sweeping shape,the heart of it facing outward;while right arm turns outward and to raise to side of body,at shoulder level,heart of palm facing upward.Eyes on right palm.(Fig.165)

☯ Using ball of right foot as pivot,turn right heel outward,the body turns to left,both palms follow the movement of body to stroke horizontally to left,to front of the body. (Fig.166)

167 上体继续左转，左脚后撤一步，脚尖外展落地，右腿屈弓；两掌心斜相对，右掌高与头平，左掌置于右肘内侧；目视右掌。

168 上体继续左转，重心左移，右脚跟外展，右腿自然蹬直，成左侧弓步（横裆步）；两掌向左平捋，逐渐握拳，左臂外旋，左拳向左划弧，卷收于腰间，拳心向上；右臂屈肘外旋滚压置于体前，右拳高与胸齐，拳心斜向上；目视右拳。

☯ The torso continues to turn to left,and take a step backward, with tiptoes turned outward to land on the ground,right leg is bent to bow;hearts of palms face obliquely each other,right palm at head level,while left palm rests on inside of right elbow.Eyes on right palm.(Fig.167)

☯ The torso continues to turn to left,shift weight to left, heel of right foot is turned outward,right leg straightens naturally to form a side bow step(side bow stance);both palms stroke horizontally leftward,and then slowly clench them into fists,left arm turns outward,and left fist moves arc to left, and withdraw to the part of left waist,heart of fist facing upward; right arm is bent to turn outward,to rotate and press to front of body,right fist at chest level,heart of fist facing obliquely upward.Eyes on right fist.(Figs.168A, 168B)

第三十四式　歇步擒打

Form 34　Cross-legged Step,Catch and Punch

169 上体右转，重心右移；右臂内旋屈肘上撑，右拳置于右额前，拳心向外；左臂内旋，左拳向身体左后方穿出，拳心向后；目视前方。

170 上体左转，左脚尖外展，重心前移；右拳经体侧下落卷收腰间，拳心向上；左拳变掌，向前划弧，掌心翻转向右；头随体转，目视前方。

171 右脚经左脚前向左前方盖步横落，两腿交叉屈蹲，成歇步；左掌握拳，收于腹前，拳心向下，虎口向内；右拳经左前臂上向前、向下方打出，高与腹平，拳心向上；目视右拳。

❂ The torso turns to right,shift weight to right;right arm turns inward,bend the elbow and extend it up,right fist comes to front of right forehead,heart of it facing outward;left arm turns inward,left fist threads out to rear left,heart of fist to the rear.Eyes front.(Fig.169)

❂ The torso turns to left,tiptoes of left foot turns outward, shift weight forward;right fist drops down past side of body, and then withdraw inward to the part of waist,heart of fist upward;open left fist into a palm,to move arc forward ,with the heart of left palm turned to right,head follows the movement of body.Eyes front.(Fig.170)

❂ Right foot takes a step past the front of left foot,and cross step to land sideways,while both legs are crisscrossed to crouch slowly forming a cross-legged step; clench left palm into a fist,withdraw to front of abdomen,heart of fist downward, "tiger mouth" (the part of the hand between the thumb and the index finger) inward;right fist punches out past over left forearm forward and downward,the fist at abdomen level,heart of fist upward.Eyes on right fist.(Fig.171)

第三十五式　穿掌下势
Form 35　Thread Palms and Push Down

172 上体右转，左脚收至右脚内侧；两拳变掌，右臂内旋，掌心翻转向外，掌指向左，提至胸前；左臂外旋，掌心翻转向外，掌指向左，举于身体左侧；目视左掌。

173 上体右转，右腿屈蹲，左腿向左侧伸出；两掌向上、向右划弧，经面前摆至身体右侧，掌心转向斜下，指尖斜向右上，右掌伸举于右前方，高与头平，左掌屈臂摆至右肩前，高与肩平；目视右掌。

174 右腿全蹲，左腿铺直，上体左转，成左仆步；两掌绕转，指尖转向左，经腹前顺左腿内侧向左穿出，左掌在前，掌心向右，右掌在后，掌心向左；目视左掌。

❷ The torso turns to right,withdraw left foot beside right foot;open both fists into palms,right arm turns inward,heart of palm turned outward,with fingertips pointing leftward,up to front of chest;left arm turns outward,with heart of palm turned outward,fingers pointing leftward,raising to left side of body. Eyes on left palm.(Fig.172)

❷ The torso turns to right,squat right leg with knee bent,and stretch out left leg towards left side;both palms move in an upward-rightward arc,past face to swing to right side of body,with hearts of palms turned obliquely downward,fingertips obliquely towards upper right,right palm stretches to front-right,at head level,and left palm with arm bent swings to front of right shoulder,at shoulder level.Eyes on right palm. (Fig.173)

❷ Right leg crouches fully,left leg stretches straight,the torso turns to left,to form a left crouching step;both palms go around,fingertips of both palms turned leftward,past abdomen and along inner side of left leg,to thread out,left palm is front,heart of palm facing rightward,right palm is latter, heart of palm facing leftward.Eyes on left palm.(Fig.174)

第三十六式　上步七星

Form 36　Step Up to Form the Shape of Seven Stars (to Form the Shape of Big Dipper)

175 重心前移，上体左转，左脚尖外撇，右脚尖内扣，右腿蹬直，左腿屈弓；左掌向前、向上挑起，腕高与肩平，掌心向右，指尖斜向上；右掌微向后拉，侧置于右胯旁；目视左掌。

176 右脚前上一步，脚前掌落地，成右虚步；左掌握拳，微向内收，拳心向右；右掌变拳向前、向上架起，拳心向外；两腕交叠，两拳交叉于身前，高与肩平，右拳在外，两臂撑圆；目视左拳。

☯ Shift weight forward,the torso turns to left,tiptoes of left foot turned outward,tiptoes of right foot turned inward, straighten right leg,bend left leg at knee to bow;snap left palm forward and upward,wrist at shoulder level,heart of palm facing rightward,the fingertips pointing obliquely upward; right palm pulls back slightly,to place obliquely beside right hip.Eyes on left palm.(Fig.175)

☯ Right foot takes a step forward,the ball of the right foot on the ground to form a right empty step;clench left palm into a fist and pull it a bit backward,heart of fist facing rightward;clench right palm into a fist and raise it forward and upward to block,heart of fist facing outward;both wrists cross before body,at shoulder level,right fist is outer, both arms rounded.Eyes on left fist.(Fig.176)

第三十七式　退步跨虎

Form 37　Step Back to Ride the Tiger

177 右脚向右后方撤一步，两拳变掌；目视两掌。

☯ Right foot takes a step backward to the rear-right,both fists turn into palms.Eyes on both palms.(Fig.177)

178 上体右转，重心后移；右掌向右下方划弧至右胯旁，掌心向下；左掌随身体右转划弧，掌心向右；头稍右转，目视右前方。

179 左脚稍向后收，脚前掌着地，落于右脚前，上体左转，身体略向下屈蹲；右掌向上划弧经头前再向左、向下划弧，落于左腿外侧，掌心向外；视线随身体转动，左顾右掌。

180 右脚蹬地，独立站稳，左腿前举，膝微屈，脚面展平，脚尖稍内扣；右掌向前、向上挑起，成侧立掌，腕高与肩平；左掌变勾手同时上提，举于左方，高与肩平，勾尖屈腕向下，上体左转；目视左前方。

❶ The torso turns to right,shift weight backward;right palm moves an arc to lower-right to the side of right hip,with heart of palm facing downward;left palm follows the body to turn to right in a curve,heart of palm facing rightward,head turns to right slightly.Eyes front-right.(Fig.178)

❶ Withdraw left foot backward slightly,the ball of the left foot on the ground,dropping down before right foot,the torso turns to left,the body squats down a bit;right palm moves in an upward curve past face and then in a leftward-downward curve down to outer side of left leg,heart of palm facing outward,line of vision follows the movement of body.Glancing right palm. (Fig.179)

❶ Straighten right foot on the ground,stand one leg firmly,and lift left leg forward,with knee bent a bit,the instep extending flat,tiptoes of left foot pointing a bit inward;right palm snaps forward and upward,to form a side standing palm,with the wrist at shoulder level;turn left palm into a hooked hand while raise it up to left,at shoulder level,tip of the hooked hand facing downward with wrist bent,the torso turns to left.Eyes front-left.(Fig.180)

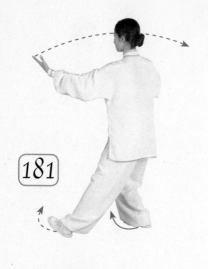

第三十八式　转身摆莲

Form 38　Turn Round and Kick Horizontally(Kick Imitating Lotus Shape)

181 左脚前落，脚跟先着地，脚尖内扣，上体右转；右臂内旋，右掌翻转向下，屈肘向右平带；左勾手变掌，掌心转向上，自后向前平摆至体侧；头随体转，目视前方。

182 以两脚前掌为轴，向右后转体；左掌摆至体前，掌心向上，高与头平，右掌翻转向上，经胸前及左肘下方向左穿出；头随体转，目视前方。

183 上体继续右转，重心坐于左腿，右脚尖虚点地面，成右虚步，右掌穿出后向上、向右划弧，置于身体右侧，腕高与肩平；左掌自右臂内侧翻转下落，收至右肩前下方，掌心亦向右；目视右掌。

❧ Left foot drops forward,heel on the ground first,with tiptoes turned inward,the torso turns to right;right arm turns inward,with palm turned downward,to bend the elbow and withdraw back horizontally to right;while open the hooked hand into a palm,with heart of palm turned upward,and swing horizontally from the rear to front to the left side of body;head follows the movement of body.Eyes front.(Fig.181)

❧ Use balls of both feet as pivot,turn body towards the rear-right;left palm swings to front of body,heart of palm facing upward,at head level,right palm is turned upward,and thread out leftward past the front of chest and under left elbow;head follows the movement of body.Eyes front.(Fig.182)

❧ The torso continues to turn to right,shift weight onto left leg,tiptoes of right foot touches on the ground, to form a right empty step, after right palm threads out,move in an upward and rightward arc,placing right side of body,wrist at shoulder level;while left palm from the inner side of right arm,turns down,and withdraw it to lower-front of right shoulder,the heart of palm also towards rightward,Eyes on right palm.(Fig.183)

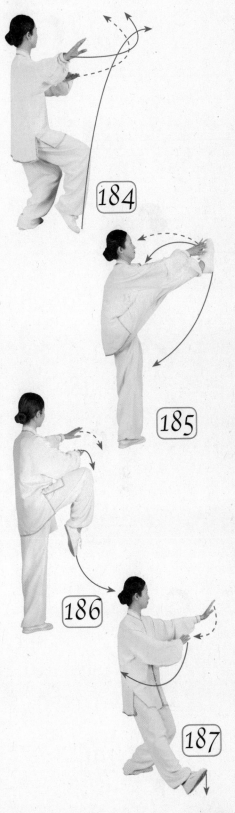

184 上体左转，右脚跟提起。

185 上体继续左转，右脚提起向左、向上、向右作扇形外摆，脚面展平；上体左转，两掌自右向左平摆，在头前左先右后依次击拍右脚面；目视两掌。

◉ The torso turns to left,right heel is raised.(Fig.184)

◉ The torso continues to turn to left,right foot raises up and in a leftward-upward-rightward fan-shaped to swing out,the instep extends flat;the torso turns to left,both palms from right to left swing horizontally at front of head to pat instep of right foot with left palm first and right palm followed.Eyes on both palms.(Fig.185)

第三十九式　弯弓射虎

Form 39　Withdraw Bow to Shoot Tiger

186 右小腿屈收，右腿屈膝提于体前侧，脚尖下垂，左腿独立站稳；上体左转，两掌继续左摆，左掌摆至身体左侧，右掌摆至左肩前下方，掌心均向下，高与肩平；目视左掌。

187 右脚向右前方落步，上体右转；两掌同时划弧下落。目视两掌。

◉ Right lower-leg is withdrawn,right leg is bent at knee to raise before front side of body,tiptoes of right foot point downward,left leg stands independently and steady;while the torso turns to left,both palms continue to swing leftward,left palm swings to left side of body ,right palm swings to left shoulder lower front,with hearts of palms facing completely downward,at shoulder level. Eyes on left palm.(Fig.186)

◉ Right foot lands on the ground to front-right,the torso turns to right;while both palms move down in a curve. Eyes on both palms.(Fig.187)

188 重心前移，两掌向下、向右划弧至身体右侧时握拳，目视右拳。

189 上体左转，右腿屈弓，成右弓步；左拳经面前向左前方打出，高与鼻平，拳心斜向前，右拳同时屈肘向左前方打出，至右额前，拳心向外；目视左拳。

☯ Shift weight forward,both palms move in a downward-rightward curve to right side of body while they are clenched into fists,Eyes on right fist.(Fig.188)

☯ The torso turns to left,bend right leg to form a right bow step;left fist strikes past face forward to left,at nose level,heart of the fist facing obliquely forward,right fist with elbow bent strikes towards front-left,to the front of right forehead,heart of fist facing outward,Eyes on left fist.(Fig.189)

第四十式　左揽雀尾
Form 40　Grasp the Bird's Tail(Left Style)

190 重心后移，右脚外撇抬起，上体右转；两拳变掌，左掌向左伸展，右掌翻转向下划弧至腰间，掌心向上，头随身体转动。

191 重心前移，左脚收至右脚内侧；右掌自下向右再翻转向上划弧，左掌由右向下划弧，两掌在胸、腹前上下合抱，掌心相对；目视右掌。

☯ Shift weight backward,right foot turned outward,and raised up,the torso turns to right;both fists turn into palms,left palm extends leftward,right palm turns downward in a curve to part of the waist,heart of palm facing upward,head follows body to move.(Fig.190)

☯ Shift weight forward,withdraw left foot beside the right foot;right palm turns from bottom to right and then turns upward in a curve,left palm moves from right to bottom in a curve,both palms close up and down before chest and abdomen,with hearts of palms facing each other.Eyes on right palm.(Fig.191)

192 上体微左转，左脚向前上步，脚跟着地；两掌微分；目视前方。

193 重心前移，左脚落实，成左弓步；左前臂向前掤出，左掌掌心向内，高与肩平；右掌按落于右胯旁，掌心向下；目视左掌。

194 上体微左转，左掌翻转向下，稍向前伸；右掌翻转向上，经腹前向上、向前划弧，伸至左前臂内侧下方；目视左掌。

195 上体右转，重心后移；两掌下捋，经腹前再向右后上方划弧，至右掌高与肩平，掌心斜向前；左掌屈臂摆至右胸前，掌心向内；目视右掌。

❧ The torso turns slightly to left,left foot takes a step forward,heel on the ground;both palms are separated a bit.Eyes front.(Fig.192)

❧ Shift weight forward,left foot sets firmly on the ground,to form a left bow step;thrust left forearm forward,with the heart of left palm facing inward,at shoulder level;right palm presses down to the side of right hip,with heart of the palm facing downward.Eyes on left palm.(Fig.193)

❧ The torso turns slightly to left,left palm turns downward and extends forward a bit;right palm turns upward,past the front of abdomen and in an upward-forward curve,and then extends below the inner part of left forearm.Eyes on left palm. (Fig.194)

❧ The torso turns to right,shift weight backward;stroke both palms down,past the front of abdomen and then move them in an upper-rear-right arc until right palm is the same level as the shoulder,heart of palm facing obliquely forward;left palm with elbow bent swings to front of right chest,heart of palm facing inward.Eyes on right palm.(Fig.195)

196 上体左转，面向前方；右掌屈臂卷收；掌指贴近左腕内侧；左臂平屈胸前，掌心向内，指尖向右；目视前方。

197 重心前移，成左弓步；双臂向前挤出，两臂撑圆，右掌指附于左腕内侧，高与肩平；目视左前臂。

198 右掌经左掌上伸出，两掌分开，与肩同宽，掌心均转向下；目视前方。

199 身体后坐，重心后移，左脚尖上翘；两臂屈肘，两掌收经胸前下落至腹前，掌心向前下方；目向前平视。

200 重心前移，成右弓步；两掌平行向上、向前按出，腕高与肩平，掌心向前，指尖向上，塌腕舒掌；目平视前方。

☯ The torso turns to left,face towards front;right palm with elbow bent is withdrawn inward;fingers rest on the inner side of left wrist;left arm is bent horizontally before chest,heart of palm facing inward,fingertips pointing rightward.Eyes front. (Fig.196)

☯ Shift weight forward to form a left bow step;both arms press out forward,and are rounded,fingers of right palm rest on the inner side.of left wrist,at shoulder level.Eyes on left forearm.(Fig.197)

☯ Right palm passes over left palm to extend,both palms are separated,with shoulder-width apart,hearts of palms turning completely downward.Eyes front.(Fig.198)

☯ Sit back,shift weight backward,tiptoes of left foot raised;both arms with elbows bent,withdraw both palms past the front of chest and then drop down to the front of abdomen,hearts of palms facing lower-front.Eyes looking straight forward. (Fig.199)

☯ Shift weight forward,to form a right bow step;both palms push out parallely upward and forward,wrist at shoulder level, hearts of palms facing forward,fingertips pointing upward, wrists relaxed and fingers apart a little. Eyes looking straight front.(Fig.200)

第四十一式 十字手
Form 41 Cross Hands

201 重心右移，上体右转，左脚尖内扣，右脚尖外展；右掌随身体右摆至面前，掌心向外；左掌分于身体左侧，掌心亦向外；目随右掌。

202 右脚尖继续外展，重心右移，上体继续右转，左腿自然蹬直；右掌摆至身体右侧，两掌左右平举于身体两侧，两肘略屈，掌心向前；目随右掌。

203 重心左移，右脚尖内扣，上体左转；两掌向下、向内划弧，于腹前两腕相交，两掌合抱，举至胸前，右掌在外，掌心均向内；目视两掌。

☯ Shift weight to right,the torso turns to right,tiptoes of left foot turn inward,tiptoes of right foot turn outward;right palm follows the body to swing towards right to the front of face,heart of palm facing outward;left palm is separated to left side of body,heart of palm is outward,too.Eyes follow right palm.(Fig.201)

☯ Tiptoes of right foot continues to turn outward,shift wight to right,the torso continues to turn to right,left leg straightens naturally;right palm swings to right side of body,both palms raise horizontally left palm to left and right palm to right and at ending both sides of body,both elbows bent a bit,hearts of palms facing forward.Eyes follow right palm. (Fig.202)

☯ Shift weight to left,tiptoes of right foot inward,the torso turns to left;both palms move in a downward-inward curve and cross wrists in front of abdomen,then raise the crossed palms to the front of chest,right palm on the outside, hearts of palms facing completely inward. Eyes on both palms.(Fig.203)

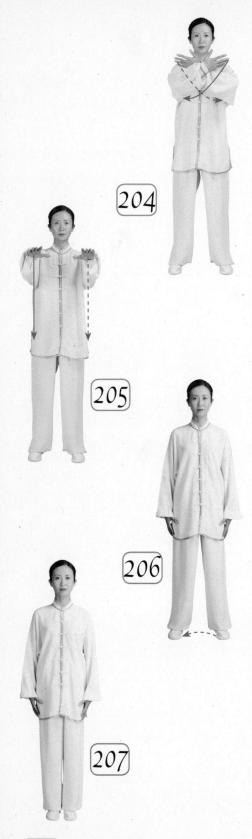

204 右脚内收，两脚与肩同宽，脚尖向前，成开立步；随即上体转正，两腿慢慢直立；两掌交叉成斜十字形抱于体前，掌心向内，高与肩平；目视两掌。

☯ Withdraw right foot beside left foot so that they are parallel with shoulder-width apart and tiptoes pointing forward,to form feet apart;and then the torso turns straight,both legs gradually stand upright;while both palms cross to a crisscross in front of body,hearts of palms facing inward,at shoulder level. Eyes on both palms.(Fig.204)

第四十二式　收势
Form 42　Closing Form

205 两前臂内旋，两掌边翻转，边平行分开，与肩同宽，掌心向前下方；目视前方。

206 两掌慢慢下落至两腿外侧，松肩垂臂，上体自然正直；目视前方。

207 左脚收至右脚旁，两脚并拢，脚尖向前，身体自然直立，呼吸平稳均匀；目视前方。

☯ Both forearms turn inward,both palms are turning and parallely separating,with shoulder-width apart,hearts of palms facing lower-front.Eyes front.(Fig.205)

☯ Both palms drop gradually to the outer side of both legs, shoulders relaxed and arms hanged,holding the torso natural erect.Eyes front.(Fig.206)

☯ Withdraw the left foot beside right foot,and then both feet are close together,tiptoes of both feet pointing forward,the body stands naturally upright,breath is even. Eyes front. (Fig.207)

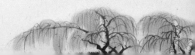

24式太极拳动作路线示意图
Movement Illustration of 24 Forms Taiji Quan

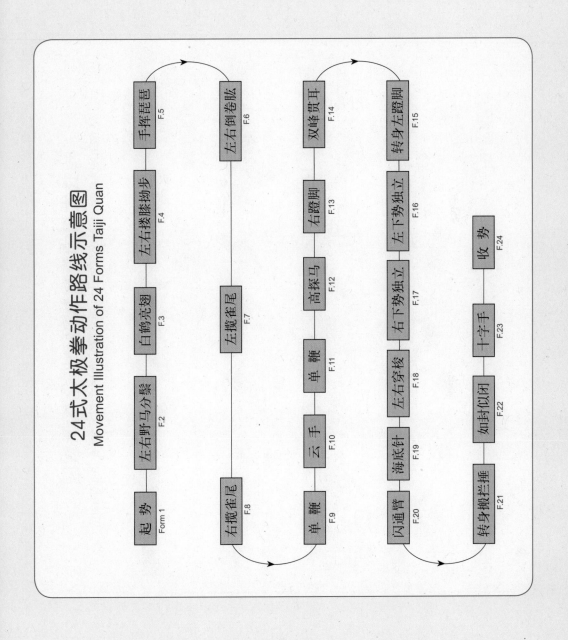

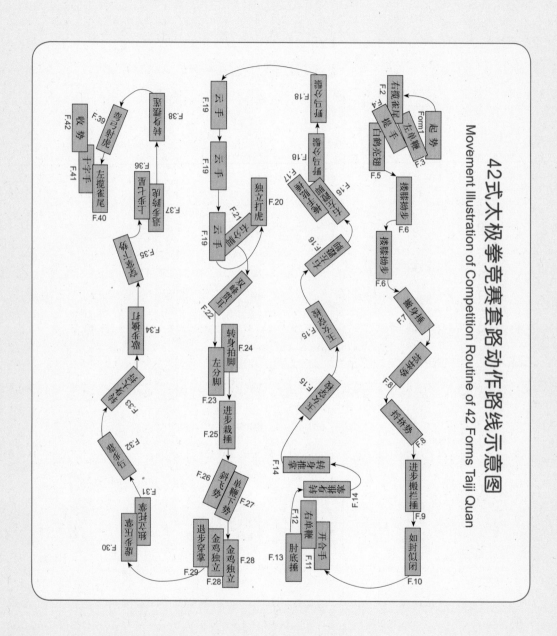

42式太极拳竞赛套路动作路线示意图

Movement Illustration of Competition Routine of 42 Forms Taiji Quan

太极拳论

武禹襄（1812--1880）名河清，河北永年人。

　　未有天地以前，太空无穷之中，浑然一气，乃为无极，无极而太极。太极者，天地之根荄，万物之原始也。太极拳者，一举动，周身俱要轻灵，尤要贯串。气宜鼓荡，神宜内敛。无使有缺陷处，无使有凸凹处，无使有断续处。其根在脚，发于腿，主宰于腰，形于手指。由脚而腿而腰，总须完整一气。向前退后，乃能得机得势。若有不得机得势处，身便散乱。其病必于腰腿间求之。上下前后左右皆然。凡此皆是在意，不在外面而在内也。有上即有下，有前即有后，有左即有右，如意要向上即寓下意。若将物掀起而加以锉之之意。斯其根自断，乃攘之速之而无疑。虚实宜分清楚。一处自有一处虚实，处处总此一虚实。周身节节贯串，无令丝毫间断耳。